T0358572

OIL PRICE
UNCERTAINTY

OIL PRICE UNCERTAINTY

Apostolos Serletis

University of Calgary, Canada

 **World Scientific**

NEW JERSEY · LONDON · SINGAPORE · BEIJING · SHANGHAI · HONG KONG · TAIPEI · CHENNAI

Published by

World Scientific Publishing Co. Pte. Ltd.

5 Toh Tuck Link, Singapore 596224

USA office: 27 Warren Street, Suite 401-402, Hackensack, NJ 07601

UK office: 57 Shelton Street, Covent Garden, London WC2H 9HE

Library of Congress Cataloging-in-Publication Data
Serletis, Apostolos.
  Oil price uncertainty / by Apostolos Serletis.
    p. c
  Includes bibliographical references and index.
  ISBN 978-9814390675
  1. Petroleum products--Prices. 2. Petroleum industry and trade--Econometric model
3. Petroleum reserves. 4. Macroeconomics. I. Titl
  HD9560.4.C37 2012
  338.2'3282--dc23
                                        2012016532

British Library Cataloguing-in-Publication Data
A catalogue record for this book is available from the British Library.

In-house Editor: Juliet Lee Ley Chin

Printed in Singapore.

To the sweetest little girl, Adia.

Contents

Preface

The relationship between the price of oil and the level of economic activity is a fundamental empirical issue in macroeconomics. As James Hamilton noted in a paper published in the *Journal of Political Economy* in 1983, at that time 7 out of 8 postwar recessions in the United States had been preceded by a sharp increase in the price of oil. More recently, in a paper published in a special issue of *Macroeconomic Dynamics* in 2011 on *Oil Price Shocks*, Hamilton continues this line of argument, by saying that "Iraq's invasion of Kuwait in August 1990 led to a doubling in the price of oil in the fall of 1990 and was followed by the ninth postwar recession in 1990-91. The price of oil more than doubled again in 1990-2000, with the tenth postwar recession coming in 2001. Yet another doubling in the price of oil in 2007-2008 accompanied the beginning of recession number 11, the most recent and frightening of the postwar economic downturns. So the count stands at 10 out of 11, the sole exception being the mild recession of 1960-61 for which there was no preceding rise in oil prices" (p. 364).

There is an ongoing debate in the macroeconomics literature about whether positive oil price shocks cause recessions in the United States (and other oil-importing countries); see, for example, Kilian (2008), Hamilton (2009), Blanchard and Riggi (2009), Edelstein and Kilian (2009), and Blanchard and Galí (2010). Those of the view that positive oil price shocks do not cause recessions appeal to theoretical models of the transmission of exogenous oil price shocks that imply symmetric responses of real output to oil price increases and decreases. These models cannot explain large declines in the level of economic activity in response to unexpected increases in the price of oil. On the other hand, those of the view that positive oil price shocks have been the major cause of recessions in the United States (and other oil-importing countries) appeal to models that imply asymmetric responses of real output to oil price increases and decreases. These models are able to explain larger recessions in response to positive oil price shocks as well as smaller expansions in response to negative ones.

Clearly, the question of how asymmetric the responses of real output are to exogenous oil price shocks is central in the debate of whether positive oil price shocks have been the major cause of recessions. Most of the empirical evidence is in support of the presence of asymmetries in the transmission of oil price shocks. Recently, however, Lutz Kilian and Robert Vigfusson (2011a) argue that this evidence is invalid. As they put it, in their paper in the special issue of *Macroeconomic Dynamics* in 2011, much of the empirical work cited in being in support of asymmetries "has not directly tested the hypothesis of an asymmetric transmission of oil price innovations. In fact, many of the papers quantifying these asymmetric responses are based on the censored oil price VAR methodology that Kilian and Vigfusson (2011b) proved to be invalid."

In this book I use recent state-of-the-art advances in macroeconometrics and financial econometrics to investigate the effects of oil price shocks and uncertainty about the price of oil on the macroeconomy. In focusing on the effects of uncertainty about the future price of oil on the level of economic activity, I abstract from other possible transmission mechanisms of exogenous oil price shocks. I present strong evidence of asymmetric responses of real output to positive and negative oil price shocks.

Of the five essays which follow, Chapters 1, 2, and 3 are new, while Chapters 4, 5, and 6 are reprints, with relatively minor revisions, of recently published work. The revisions which I have made were meant to eliminate repetitive passages and a certain amount of overlap between the individual essays.

A number of institutions and individuals have made the completion of these essays possible. I would like to thank my coauthors, John Elder and Sajjadur Rahman, of the original papers that have been reprinted in this book as Chapters 4, 5 and 6. Thanks are also due to the colleagues that commented on one or more of these essays — James Hamilton, Lutz Kilian, the Editor of the *Journal of Money, Credit and Banking*, Pok-sang Lam, the Editor of *Macroeconomic Dynamics*, William Barnett, the Editors of *Energy Economics*, Beng Ang, Richard Tol, and John Weyant, and the anonymous referees of these journals. Of course, none of them is responsible for the finished product.

Finally, I would like to thank Joanne Canape for a thoroughly professional job of preparing the camera-ready copy of this book. Without her help, this venture would not have been possible.

Chapter 1

Introduction

As noted in the *Preface*, the relationship between the price of oil and the level of economic activity is a fundamental empirical issue in macroeconomics. The theoretical literature suggests the existence of a number of *transmission mechanisms* (or *channels*) through which oil price innovations affect real output, and most of these transmission mechanisms (but not all) imply asymmetric responses of real output to oil price increases and decreases.

In what follows I discuss some of these channels through which oil price innovations affect real output.

1.1   Transmission Mechanisms

1.1.1   *The income transfer channel*

This channel emphasizes the price of imported crude oil and the change in the purchasing power of domestic households associated with increases in the real price of oil. As Rubin and Buchanan put it, in a CIBC World Markets *Report* published in 2008,

> "the transfer of income from US consumers to Saudi producers involves moving money from basically a zero-savings-rate economy to one in which the savings rate is around 50%. While many of those petro-dollars get recycled back into the financial assets of OECD countries, many of them never get spent" (p. 4).

Rubin and Buchanan continue by saying that it hasn't been only consumers in the United States that have been socked with

> "mounting fuel bills. It's been true for households from all OECD countries. Over the last five years their annual fuel bill has grown a staggering $700 billion. Of this, $400 billion annually has gone to OPEC producers" (p. 5).

It is to be noted that according to this transmission mechanism, it is the price of imported oil that is relevant; changes in the price of domestically produced oil lead to a redistribution of income, with no reduction in aggregate income. Also, the direct effect of an increase in the price of imported oil is symmetric in positive and negative oil price shocks. That is, a positive oil price shock will reduce aggregate income by as much as a negative oil price shock of the same magnitude will increase aggregate income.

Clearly, the rationale for asymmetric responses of real output to oil price increases and decreases hinges on the existence of other indirect transmission mechanisms of unexpected oil price changes, to which I now turn.

1.1.2 *The reallocation channel*

In another *Journal of Political Economy* paper in 1988, Hamilton argues that oil price shocks are relative price shocks and can cause intersectoral and intrasectoral reallocations of factors of production throughout the economy. For example, an unexpected increase in the real price of oil may reduce expenditures on energy intensive durables and cause a reallocation of capital and labor away from energy intensive industries. If capital and labor cannot be employed easily in other sectors, such reallocations will cause these factors of production to be unemployed, resulting in reduced real output beyond that from the decline in the purchasing power of households triggered by unexpectedly high oil prices.

As Kilian and Vigfusson (2011a, p. 339) put it, regarding this indirect transmission mechanism of unexpected oil price changes,

> "in the case of an unexpected real oil price increase, the reallocation effect reinforces the recessionary effects of the loss of purchasing power, allowing the model to generate a much larger recession than in standard linear models. In the case of an unexpected real oil price decline, the reallocation effect partially offsets the increased expenditures driven by the gains in purchasing power, causing a smaller economic expansion than implied by a linear model. This means that in the presence of a reallocation effect, the responses of real output are necessarily asymmetric in unanticipated oil price increases and unanticipated oil price decreases."

1.1.3 *The monetary policy response channel*

Another explanation for asymmetric responses of real output to oil price innovations focuses on how monetary policy responds to oil price shocks — see, for example, Bernanke *et al.* (1997). According to this channel, an unexpected increase in the price of oil leads to an increase in the price level, thereby reducing real money balances held by households and firms. The decline in real money balances leads to a decline in aggregate demand through traditional monetary policy effects, such as the *interest rate effect* and the *exchange rate effect*.

For example, the decline in real money balances leads to an increase in real interest rates, which in turn increases the cost of capital, causing a fall in investment spending, thereby leading to a decline in aggregate demand and a decline in output. In addition to interest rate effects, this channel also involves exchange rate effects. In particular, the increase in real interest rates leads to an appreciation of the domestic currency, making domestic goods more expensive than foreign goods, thereby causing a fall in net exports and hence in aggregate demand.

The premise is that the central bank responds to such inflationary pressures associated with unexpected increases in the price of oil by raising the interest rate. This in turn amplifies the economic contraction. Also, the asymmetry arises because the central bank responds vigorously to positive oil price shocks, but does not respond as vigorously to negative oil price shocks.

Regarding this explanation for asymmetric responses of real output to oil price innovations, in the past, when oil prices rose prior to recessions so did interest rates, and as has been argued by Bernanke *et al.* (1997) it was the increase in the interest rate that led to the downturn. However, this view has been challenged by Hamilton and Herrera (2004), who argue that contractionary monetary policy plays only a secondary role in generating the contractions in real output and that it is the increase in the oil price that directly leads to contractions. See also Herrera and Pesavento (2009) and Kilian and Lewis (2011) regarding the 'fragile' empirical evidence in support of the monetary policy response channel.

1.1.4   *The uncertainty channel*

Finally, another indirect transmission mechanism of unexpected oil price changes, focuses on the effects of uncertainty about the price of oil in the future on investment spending. In particular, according to the *real options theory*, also known as investment under uncertainty, uncertainty about the future price of oil will cause firms to delay production and investments. The theoretical foundations of real options are provided by Bernanke (1983), Brennan and Schwartz (1985), Majd and Pindyck (1987), and Brennan (1990), among others.

For example, an increase in the uncertainty about the future price of oil will reduce investment spending that has uncertain future return, is costly to reverse, and for which there is flexibility in timing, thereby leading to a decline in output. In fact, many firm expenditures fall in this category, including fixed investment in large manufacturing facilities (i.e., an automobile plant), investment associated with the hiring and training of labor, investment in equipment that does not have a well functioning secondary market, and investment in energy intensive (i.e., manufacturing) and energy extensive (i.e., mining) industries.

The idea is that the uncertainty effect amplifies the negative effects of positive oil price shocks and also offsets the positive effects of negative oil price shocks, resulting in asymmetric responses of real output to oil price innovations, much like the reallocation effect.

1.2 Testing for Nonlinearity

Most of the empirical work cited as being in support of asymmetric responses of real output to oil price shocks is based on 'slope-based' tests of the null hypothesis of linearity.

Let y_t denote the growth rate of real output ($y_t = \Delta \ln Output_t$) and x_t that of the real or nominal price of oil ($x_t = \Delta \ln Oil_t$). In the context of a forecasting regression, testing the null hypothesis that the optimal one-period ahead forecast of y_t is linear in past values of x_t involves estimating (by ordinary least squares) the following regression

$$y_t = \alpha_0 + \sum_{j=1}^{p} \alpha_j y_{t-j} + \sum_{j=1}^{p} \beta_j x_{t-j} + \sum_{j=1}^{p} \gamma_j \tilde{x}_{t-j} + \varepsilon_t \qquad (1.1)$$

where α_0, α_j, β_j, and γ_j are all parameters, ε_t is white noise, and $\tilde{x}_t$ is a known nonlinear function of oil prices. In equation (1.1), testing for nonlinearity is equivalent to testing the null hypothesis that the coefficients on the nonlinear measure, $\tilde{x}_t$, are all equal to zero — that is, $\gamma_1 = \gamma_2 = \cdots = \gamma_p = 0$. If the joint null of linearity and symmetry in the coefficients can be rejected, then the conclusion is that the relationship is nonlinear.

Mork (1989) was the first to censor the oil price change to exclude all oil price decreases and test the joint null hypothesis of linearity and symmetry, after the dramatic decline in oil prices in the mid 1980s failed to lead to a boom in output growth. In particular, in the context of (1.1), he proposed the following nonlinear transformation of the (real) price of oil

$$\tilde{x}_t = \max \{0, o_t - o_{t-1}\} \qquad (1.2)$$

where o_t is the logarithm of the real price of oil. Mork showed that oil price increases preceded an economic contraction, but he could not reject the null hypothesis that declines in the price of oil did not lead to economic expansions.

Hamilton (1996) refined this approach and captured nonlinearities in the nominal price of oil by the 'net oil price increase' over the previous 12 months (so as to filter out increases in the price of oil that represent corrections for recent declines)

$$\tilde{x}_t = \max\left\{0,\ o_t - \max\left\{o_{t-1}, \cdots, o_{t-12}\right\}\ \right\} \qquad (1.3)$$

with o_t in this case denoting the logarithm of the nominal price of oil ($o_t = \ln Oil_t$). He found that sustained increases in oil prices have more predictive content for real output than transitory fluctuations. Hamilton (2003) reaffirmed this finding, by focusing on net oil price changes over the previous 36 months

$$\tilde{x}_t = \max\left\{0,\ o_t - \max\left\{o_{t-1}, \cdots, o_{t-36}\right\}\ \right\}. \qquad (1.4)$$

A large number of papers have tested the joint null of linearity and symmetry in the slope coefficients of the predictive regression (1.1) and rejected it. For example, Hamilton (2011) builds on Hamilton's (1996, 2003) analysis of the postwar period, and after extending the sample period to include the recent Great Recession, he concludes that the evidence is convincing that the predictive relation between GDP growth and nominal oil prices is nonlinear.

Also, Herrera *et al.* (2011) investigate whether the oil price-output relation is nonlinear by testing the null hypothesis of linearity (and symmetry) in the context of the reduced form (1.1), using monthly United States data on oil prices and 37 industrial production indices (of which 5 represent aggregates). In doing so, they use Mork's oil price increase, as defined by equation (1.2), Hamilton's (1996) net oil price increase over the previous 12 months, as defined by equation (1.3), as well as Hamilton's (2003) net oil price increase over the previous 36 months, as defined by equation (1.4). They reject the null hypothesis of linearity (and symmetry) for a large number of industrial production indices with the evidence against the null appearing stronger when the net oil price increase over the previous 36 months is used.

Finally, recent work by Kilian and Vigfusson (2011a) shows that substantively identical test results are obtained for the real price of oil in the sample period since 1973. That finding holds even using a 'modified' slope-based test developed in Kilian and Vigfusson (2011b) that includes additional contemporaneous regressors in model (1.1). In particular, this modified test is based on the following structural equation

$$y_t = \alpha_0 + \sum_{j=1}^{p} \alpha_j y_{t-j} + \sum_{j=0}^{p} \beta_j x_{t-j} + \sum_{j=0}^{p} \gamma_j \tilde{x}_{t-j} + \varepsilon_t \qquad (1.5)$$

and testing the joint null hypothesis of linearity and symmetry involves testing the null that the coefficients on the nonlinear measure, $\tilde{x}_t$, are all equal to zero — in this case, $\gamma_0 = \gamma_1 = \cdots = \gamma_p = 0$. Kilian and Vigfusson reject the null hypothesis although with slightly larger p-values than Hamilton does. Herrera *et al.* (2011) also report results based on the structural equation (1.5) that are very similar to their results based on the reduced form (1.1).

Thus, there is a consensus that slope-based tests generally support the view that the predictive relationship between the price of oil and U.S. real output is nonlinear.

1.3 Nonlinearity versus Asymmetry

The evidence of nonlinearity based on slope-based tests (either the traditional or the modified ones) has so far been taken as being in support of an asymmetric relation between the price of oil and real output. Recently, however, Kilian and Vigfusson (2011b) argue that slope-based tests focus on the wrong null hypothesis and propose a direct test of the null hypothesis of symmetric impulse responses to positive and negative oil price shocks based on impulse response functions (rather than slopes), arguing that this is the hypothesis of interest to economists. The idea is that asymmetric slopes are neither necessary nor sufficient for asymmetric responses of real output to positive and negative oil price shocks. As Kilian and Vigfusson (2011b, p. 436-437) put it,

> "what is at issue in conducting this impulse-response-based test is not the existence of asymmetries in the reduced form parameters, but the question of whether possible asymmetries in the reduced form imply significant asymmetries in the impulse response function."

In particular, slope-based tests are not informative with respect to whether the asymmetry in the impulse responses is economically or statistically significant. This is because impulse response functions are nonlinear functions of the slope parameters and innovation variances and it is possible for small and statistically insignificant departures from symmetry in the slopes to cause large and statistically significant departures from symmetry in the implied impulse response functions. Similarly, it is possible for large and statistically significant departures from symmetry in the slopes to cause small and statistically insignificant departures from symmetry in the implied impulse response functions. In addition, Kilian and Vigfusson argue that slope-based tests of symmetry cannot allow for the fact that the degree of asymmetry of the response function by construction depends on the magnitude of the shock. In other words, the degree of asymmetry may differ greatly for an oil price innovation of typical magnitude (say, one standard deviation) compared with large oil price innovations (say, two-standard deviation shocks).

Kilian and Vigfusson (2011b) investigate whether the impulse responses of U.S. real GDP over the post-1973 period are asymmetric to oil price increases and decreases and find no evidence against the null hypothesis of symmetric response functions. Also, Kilian and Vigfusson (2011) extend the sample period to include the Great Recession and find no evidence against the null hypothesis of symmetry in the case of shocks of typical magnitude. However, they find statistically significant evidence of nonlinearity when they examine the effects of large (two standard deviation) shocks and discuss the possibility that this evidence could be an artifact of the simultaneous occurrence of the financial crisis

Herrera *et al.* (2011) also use the Kilian and Vigfusson (2011b) impulse-response based test and reject the null hypothesis of symmetric impulse responses with both aggregate and disaggregate monthly industrial production series, for both typical and large shocks, in samples that include pre-1970s data. However, for the post-1973 period they find no evidence against the null of symmetry at the aggregate level, consistent with the results by Kilian and Vigfusson (2011b) for aggregate real GDP, but continue to find some evidence at the disaggregate level in response to large shocks.

Thus, based on the Kilian and Vigfusson (2011b) impulse-response function tests, it appears that for shocks of typical magnitude the nonlinearities in the impulse-response functions are immaterial.

1.4   Modeling Uncertainty

In this book, I focus on the effects of uncertainty about the future price of oil on the level of economic activity and abstract from other possible direct and indirect effects of oil price changes.

Uncertainty is a very important concept in economics and finance, perhaps the most important, and has been the subject of a vast theoretical and empirical literature. As noted by Campbell *et al.* (1997, p. 3),

> "what distinguishes financial economics is the central role that uncertainty plays in both financial theory and its empirical implementation. The starting point for every financial model is the uncertainty facing investors, and the substance of every financial model involves the impact of uncertainty on the behavior of investors and, ultimately, on market prices. Indeed, in the absence of uncertainty, the problems of financial economics reduce to exercises in basic microeconomics."

In empirical implementations, uncertainty is usually measured by the volatility of the price of an asset (or good). In this section, I briefly discuss some methods and econometric models available in the literature for modeling oil price volatility. For more details, see Andersen *et al.* (2006).

1.4.1 *Historical volatility*

The simplest volatility model is the historical estimate. In the context of oil prices, it involves the calculation of the variance, σ^2, or standard deviation, σ, of oil price returns over some period and using it as the volatility forecast for all periods in the future.

1.4.2 *Stochastic volatility*

A simple example of stochastic volatility is autoregressive volatility. The basic idea is to calculate a time series on some volatility proxy, assume that it is a stochastic process, and then apply standard autoregressive (AR) or autoregressive-moving average (ARMA) models to obtain volatility forecasts.

For example, in the case of daily volatility, one might use daily squared returns or daily range estimators, the latter calculated as the logarithm of the ratio of the highest observed price to the lowest observed price,

$$\sigma^2 = \ln(\text{High}/\text{Low}),$$

as the volatility estimate for a given day. Using either daily squared returns or the daily range estimator, a daily time series of observations on that volatility proxy is then constructed and volatility forecasts can be obtained by fitting standard time series models to that time series. In the case, for example, of an AR(q) model

$$\sigma_t^2 = w + \sum_{j=1}^{q} \beta_j \sigma_{t-j}^2 + \varepsilon_t, \qquad (1.6)$$

the parameters, $w, \beta_1, \cdots, \beta_q$, can be estimated (using either ordinary least squares or maximum likelihood methods), and volatility forecasts could be produced.

By assuming that the volatility of the underlying price is a stochastic process, rather than a constant (as is the case with historical volatility), stochastic volatility models are popular in mathematical finance and in the valuation of derivative securities, such as options.

1.4.3   *Implied volatility*

In finance, all options pricing models require a volatility estimate as an input. Consider, for example, the standard Black and Scholes (1973) option pricing model which gives the following mathematical formula for the value of a call option

$$C = SN(d_1) - Xe^{-R_f T} N(d_2)$$

with

$$d_1 = \frac{\log(\frac{S}{X}) + [R_f + .5\sigma^2]T}{\sigma T^{1/2}}$$

$$d_2 = \frac{\log(\frac{S}{X}) + [R_f - .5\sigma^2]T}{\sigma T^{1/2}} = d_1 - \sigma T^{1/2}$$

where $e = 2.7128$ and $N(d)$ is the probability that a normally distributed random variable will take on a value less than or equal to d. S is the current price of the underlying asset, X the exercise (or strike) price of the option, R_f is the risk-free interest rate, σ is the standard deviation of the asset's returns, and T is the time to expiration of the option.

Using such an option pricing model and (available) information on the five key determinants of the option's price (asset price, strike price, volatility, time to expiration, and risk-free rate), it is possible to determine the volatility forecast over the lifetime of the option implied by the option's valuation. Thus, implied volatility is the volatility of the price of the underlying asset that is implied by the market price of the option based on an option pricing model. It is a forward-looking measure of volatility, unlike historical volatility which is calculated from known past returns of an asset.

1.4.4 *Conditional volatility*

Interest in conditional volatility modeling has been spurred by the AutoRegressive Conditional Heteroscedasticity (ARCH) model, developed by Engle (1982), the co-winner of the 2003 Nobel Memorial Prize in Economic Sciences. The basic idea is to model (and forecast) volatility as a time-varying function of current information, by assuming that a stochastic variable, x_t, has time-dependent variance (hence the term 'heteroscedasticity,' as opposed to 'homoscedasticity').

In particular, in a univariate formulation, the ARCH model is defined by

$$x_t = \phi_0 + \sum_{j=1}^{s} \phi_j x_{t-j} + \varepsilon_t \tag{1.7}$$

where $\varepsilon_t \mid \Omega_{t-1} \sim D\left(0, \sigma_t^2\right)$, Ω_{t-1} is the information set, and

$$\sigma_t^2 = w + \sum_{i=1}^{p} \alpha_i \varepsilon_{t-i}^2. \tag{1.8}$$

Equation (1.7) is the conditional mean equation and describes how the dependent variable, x_t, changes over time. In equation (1.7), s is the order of the autoregression, $\phi_0, \phi_1, \cdots, \phi_s$ are unknown parameters to be estimated, and the error term ε_t is assumed to be distributed according to some distribution D with zero mean and (changing) variance σ_t^2.

Equation (1.8) is the conditional variance equation and describes how the conditional variance of the error term in (1.7), σ_t^2, varies over time. According to (1.8), σ_t^2 is an autoregressive process of the squared residuals, hence the term 'autoregressive conditional heteroscedasticity.' In equation (1.8), $w_0 > 0, \alpha_1, \cdots, \alpha_p \geq 0$ are unknown coefficients — they are non-negative in order to avoid the possibility of negative conditional variances. If these coefficients are positive, then the ARCH model predicts that large squared innovations in the recent past will lead to a large current squared innovation, in the sense that its conditional variance, σ_t^2, will be large; for $p = 0$, ε_t is simply white noise (that is, a zero mean, constant variance, and serially uncorrelated process).

Thus, in the case of oil prices (and of economic and financial time series in general), it makes sense to use conditional volatility models which do not assume that the variance of the errors is constant and describe how that variance evolves. These models are designed to deal with *volatility clustering*, noted by Mandelbrot (1963), the observation that large price changes tend to be followed by large changes, positive or negative, and small price changes tend to be followed by small ones.

1.5   Tests of the Uncertainty Effect

Although there exists a vast literature that investigates the effects of oil price shocks, there are relatively few studies that investigate the direct effects of uncertainty about oil prices on the real economy.

One of the early papers to model oil price uncertainty was Lee *et al.* (1995), using ARCH-type models. In particular, (abstracting from nonessential variables) they used the following *univariate* generalized ARCH (also known as GARCH) process for the rate of change in the price of oil, x_t,

$$x_t = \phi_0 + \sum_{j=1}^{s} \phi_j x_{t-j} + \varepsilon_t$$

where $\varepsilon_t \mid \Omega_{t-1} \sim N\left(0, \sigma_t^2\right)$, Ω_{t-1} is the information set, and

$$\sigma_t^2 = w + \sum_{j=1}^{q} \beta_j \sigma_{t-j}^2 + \sum_{i=1}^{p} \alpha_i \varepsilon_{t-i}^2.$$

The conditional expectation of the rate of change in the price of oil is $\hat{x}_t = E(x_t \mid \Omega_{t-1})$ and the forecast error is $\varepsilon_t = x_t - \hat{x}_t$. Because the forecast error, ε_t, does not reflect changes in conditional volatility over time, Lee *et al.* (1995) calculated the following measure of an unexpected oil price shock that reflects both the magnitude and the variability of the forecast error

$$\varepsilon_t^* = \frac{\varepsilon_t}{\sqrt{\sigma_t^2}}.$$

Lee *et al.* (1995) then (treated the price of oil as exogenous and) introduced ε_t^* in various VAR systems, and found that oil price volatility is highly significant in explaining economic growth. They also found evidence of asymmetry, in the sense that positive oil price shocks have a strong effect on growth while negative oil price shocks do not. The Lee *et al.* (1995) tests, however, are subject to the generated regressor problem, described by Pagan (1984).

1.6   Scope and Strategy

In this book, I use recent advances in the theory and practice of *multivariate volatility* models to investigate the relationship between the price of oil and the level of economic activity, focusing on the role of uncertainty about oil prices. I utilize a fully specified bivariate framework, based on both structural (in Chapter 4) and reduced form (in Chapters 5 and 6) VARs that are modified to accommodate GARCH-in-Mean errors. I abstract from other possible transmission mechanisms of oil price shocks, treat the price of oil as predetermined with respect to real economic activity, and estimate the models on post-1973 data for the United States (in Chapters 4 and 5) and Canada (in Chapter 6).

As a measure of uncertainty about the price of oil, I use the conditional standard deviation of the forecast error for the change in the price of oil. I also investigate how accounting for oil price uncertainty affects the response of output to an oil price shock, by simulating impulse-response functions for the bivariate GARCH-in-Mean structural and reduced form VARs. I make the case that we need to control for the separate effects of oil price volatility in assessing the effects of oil prices on macroeconomic performance. I also investigate the robustness of the results to

   i) alternative measures of the price of oil,
   ii) alternative measures of the level of economic activity, and
   iii) alternative data frequencies and model specifications.

Without providing a formal test of the symmetry of the impulse response functions, as Kilian and Vigfusson (2011b) do, I present strong evidence of asymmetric responses of real output to positive and negative oil price shocks. In fact, the main findings are the following:

   i) uncertainty about the price of oil tends to cause real output growth to decline,
   ii) the responses of real output to positive and negative oil price shocks are asymmetric,
   iii) accounting for oil price uncertainty tends to amplify the dynamic negative response of real output to an unfavorable (positive) oil price shock,
   iv) accounting for oil price uncertainty tends to dampen the dynamic positive response of real output to a favorable (negative) oil price shock.

What follows could be viewed as a progress report on the fascinating relationship between the price of oil and the level of economic activity, based on the use of recent advances in macroeconometrics and financial econometrics. As Kilian and Vigfusson (2011a, p. 355) put it, "further studies using updated time series data and state-of-the-art methods of estimation and inference appear promising avenues for research."

Chapter 2

Univariate Volatility Models

2.1   Introduction

In recent years, economists and finance theorists have been creating new models and tools that can capture important nonlinearities in economic and financial data. One reason for their interest in these methods is what one might call the *forecasting paradox* — the fact that linear models produce invariably good in-sample fits, but usually fail miserably at out-of-sample prediction. Economists are therefore tempted to explore means by which apparent dependencies in the residuals of linear models (that are inconsistent with a linear data generator) can be exploited to produce better forecasts.

In fact, recent leading-edge research in economics and finance has applied the autoregressive conditional heteroscedasticity (ARCH) model, developed by Engle (1982) to estimate time-varying variances in commodity prices. Other models include Bollerslev's (1986) generalized ARCH (GARCH) model and Nelson's (1991) exponential GARCH (EGARCH) model. Since most economic and financial time series are nonstationary, nonlinear, and time-varying, one would achieve superior modeling using such parametric nonlinear time series models in which the unconditional variance is constant but the conditional variance, like the conditional mean, is also a random variable depending on current and past information.

This chapter is devoted to univariate time series models in which stochastic variables are assumed to have a time-dependent variance (and are called *heteroscedastic*, as opposed to *homoscedastic*). These models are designed to model and forecast the conditional variance (or volatility) of the dependent variable.

2.2   ARCH and Related Models

2.2.1   *The ARCH Model*

A model that can be used to explain the tendency of large residuals to cluster together is the autoregressive conditional heteroscedasticity (ARCH) model, developed by Engle (1982)

$$y_t = \phi_0 + \sum_{j=1}^{s} \phi_j y_{t-j} + \varepsilon_t \tag{2.1}$$

$$\varepsilon_t \, | \, \Omega_t \sim D(0, \sigma_t^2)$$

$$\sigma_t^2 = w + \sum_{i=1}^{p} \alpha_i \varepsilon_{t-i}^2 \qquad (2.2)$$

Equation (2.1) is the conditional mean equation (referred to as the *mean model*) and describes how the dependent variable, y_t, changes over time. In equation (2.1), s is the order of the autoregression, ϕ are unknown parameters to be estimated, and the error term ε_t is assumed to be distributed according to some distribution D with zero mean and (changing) variance σ_t^2. In many finance applications the mean model is just the intercept, ϕ_0, but here we model the dependent variable, y_t, as an autoregressive (AR) process of order s or simply an AR(s) process.

Equation (2.2) is the conditional variance equation (referred to as the *variance model*) and describes how the conditional variance of the error term in equation (2.1), σ_t^2, varies over time. According to (2.2), σ_t^2 is an autoregressive process of the squared residuals, hence the term *autoregressive conditional heteroscedasticity*. In equation (2.2), $w > 0, \alpha_1, \cdots, \alpha_p \geq 0$ are unknown coefficients — they are non-negative in order to avoid the possibility of negative conditional variances. If these coefficients are positive, then the ARCH model predicts that large squared innovations in the recent past will lead to a large current squared innovation, in the sense that its conditional variance, σ_t^2, will be large; for $p = 0$, ε_t is simply white noise (that is, a zero mean, constant variance, and serially uncorrelated process).

Although we apply the ARCH model to the error variance of the AR(s) model for y_t given by equation (2.1), it should be noted that the ARCH model can be applied to the error variance of any time series regression model (with an error term that has a conditional mean of zero), including time series models with multiple predictors.

2.2.2 The GARCH Model

An extension of the ARCH model is the generalized ARCH, or GARCH, model proposed by Bollerslev (1986). In the generalized ARCH(p, q) model — called GARCH(p, q) — σ_t^2 depends on lagged (squared) residuals as well as on its own lags. The conditional mean and variance equations of the AR(s)-GARCH(q, p) model are as follows

$$y_t = \phi_0 + \sum_{j=1}^{s} \phi_j y_{t-j} + \varepsilon_t$$

$$\varepsilon_t \,|\Omega_t \sim D(0, \sigma_t^2)$$

$$\sigma_t^2 = w + \sum_{j=1}^{q} \beta_j \sigma_{t-j}^2 + \sum_{i=1}^{p} \alpha_i \varepsilon_{t-i}^2 \qquad (2.3)$$

and $w > 0, \alpha_1, \cdots, \alpha_p, \beta_1, \cdots, \beta_q \geq 0$ are unknown coefficients — they are non-negative in order to avoid the possibility of negative conditional variances. Hence, the (changing) conditional variance of ε_t, σ_t^2, looks very much like an ARMA(p, q) process in the $\left\{\varepsilon_t^2\right\}$ sequence. In fact, this is the key feature of GARCH models — they allow the conditional variance of the disturbances of the $\{y_t\}$ sequence to be an ARMA process.

In equation (2.3), the sizes of the α and β coefficients determine the short-run dynamics of the conditional variance, σ_t^2. In particular, large β coefficients indicate that volatility is *persistent*, since shocks to the conditional variance take a long time to die out. Large α coefficients indicate that volatility reacts intensely to y_t movements — in fact, if α is relatively high and β is relatively low then volatility tends to be more *spiky*.

It is also to be noted that by incorporating lags of the conditional variance, the GARCH model can capture slowly changing volatility with fewer parameters than the ARCH model. In fact, it is rarely necessary to use more than a GARCH(1,1) model, as follows

$$\sigma_t^2 = w + \beta \sigma_{t-1}^2 + \alpha \varepsilon_{t-1}^2$$

with $w > 0, \alpha, \beta \geq 0$. This model can be written as

$$\begin{aligned}
\sigma_t^2 &= w + \beta \sigma_{t-1}^2 + \alpha \varepsilon_{t-1}^2 \\
&= w + \alpha \varepsilon_{t-1}^2 + \beta \left(w + \alpha \varepsilon_{t-2}^2 + \beta \left(w + \alpha \varepsilon_{t-3}^2 + \beta(\cdots)\right)\right) \\
&= \frac{w}{1 - \beta} + \alpha \left(\varepsilon_{t-1}^2 + \beta \varepsilon_{t-2}^2 + \beta^2 \varepsilon_{t-3}^2 + \cdots\right)
\end{aligned}$$

suggesting that the GARCH(1,1) model is equivalent to an infinite ARCH model with exponentially declining weights.

2.2.3 *The Exponential GARCH Model*

Nelson (1991) developed a number of alternatives to the GARCH model. The first is called exponential GARCH, or EGARCH, and models the log of the variance, rather than the level. The conditional mean and conditional variance equations for the standard AR(s)-EGARCH(q, p) model are as follows

$$y_t = \phi_0 + \sum_{j=1}^{s} \phi_j y_{t-j} + \varepsilon_t$$

$$\varepsilon_t \,|\Omega_t \sim D(0, \sigma_t^2)$$

$$\ln\left(\sigma_t^2\right) = w + \sum_{j=1}^{q} \beta_j \ln(\sigma_{t-j}^2) + \sum_{i=1}^{p} \alpha_i \left|\frac{\varepsilon_{t-i}}{\sqrt{\sigma_{t-i}^2}}\right|. \quad (2.4)$$

Note that the log transformation ensures that σ_t^2 remains non-negative for all t and that forecasts of the conditional variance are guaranteed to be nonnegative.

The models discussed so far do not capture *asymmetry effects*, where positive values of the residuals have different effects than negative ones, because the residuals enter the variance equation either as a square or absolute value. The standard EGARCH model can also be modified to introduce asymmetrical conditional variance effects by adding an extra term to the variance equation as follows

$$\ln\left(\sigma_t^2\right) = w + \sum_{j=1}^{q} \beta_j \ln(\sigma_{t-j}^2) + \sum_{i=1}^{p} \alpha_i \left|\frac{\varepsilon_{t-i}}{\sqrt{\sigma_{t-i}^2}}\right| + \sum_{k=1}^{r} \gamma_k \frac{\varepsilon_{t-k}}{\sqrt{\sigma_{t-k}^2}}. \quad (2.5)$$

In (2.5), the logged conditional variance, $\ln\left(\sigma_t^2\right)$, depends on both the size and the sign of lagged residuals. In this setup if $\gamma_k \neq 0$, the news impact is asymmetric; for example, if $\gamma_k > 0$, negative shocks (bad news) will cause volatility to rise by more than positive shocks (good news) of the same magnitude and we say that there is a *leverage effect* for the kth order. Thus, the presence of leverage effects can be tested by the null hypothesis that $\gamma_k < 0$; the effect is asymmetric if $\gamma_k \neq 0$.

2.2.4 *The Integrated GARCH Model*

Another model, also due to Nelson (1991), is the integrated GARCH (IGARCH) model. It restricts the parameters in the variance equation of the GARCH model to sum to one and drops the constant term, w, as follows

$$y_t = \phi_0 + \sum_{j=1}^{s} \phi_j y_{t-j} + \varepsilon_t$$

$$\varepsilon_t \,|\, \Omega_t \sim D(0, \sigma_t^2)$$

$$\sigma_t^2 = \sum_{j=1}^{q} \beta_j \sigma_{t-j}^2 + \sum_{i=1}^{p} \alpha_i \varepsilon_{t-i}^2$$

with

$$\sum_{i=1}^{p} \alpha_i + \sum_{j=1}^{q} \beta_j = 1.$$

2.2.5   The Threshold GARCH Model

The threshold GARCH (TARCH) model was introduced independently by Glosten *et al.* (1993) and Zakoïan (1994). The specifications for the conditional mean and variance equations for the standard AR(s)-TARCH(q, p) model are as follows

$$y_t = \phi_0 + \sum_{j=1}^{s} \phi_j y_{t-j} + \varepsilon_t$$

$$\varepsilon_t \,|\, \Omega_t \sim D(0, \sigma_t^2)$$

$$\sigma_t^2 = w + \sum_{j=1}^{q} \beta_j \sigma_{t-j}^2 + \sum_{i=1}^{p} \alpha_i \varepsilon_{t-i}^2 + \sum_{k=1}^{r} \gamma_k \varepsilon_{t-k}^2 I_{t-k} \qquad (2.6)$$

where

$$I_t = \begin{cases} 1, \text{ if } \varepsilon_t < 0; \\ \\ 0, \text{ otherwise.} \end{cases}$$

In this model, when the ith period's residual is positive (as in the case of good news), then $I_{t-i} = 0$ and the effect of the ith period's squared residual on the current volatility is simply α_i. When the ith period's residual is negative (as in the case of bad news), then $I_{t-i} = 1$ and the effect of the ith period's squared residual on the current volatility is $\alpha_i + \gamma_i$. Thus, in this setup if $\gamma_i \neq 0$, the news impact is asymmetric. Of course, if $\gamma = 0$, the response of volatility to shocks is symmetric, in the sense that volatility is driven only by the size (and not the sign) of shocks. Clearly, the GARCH model is a special case of the threshold GARCH model where the threshold terms are set equal to zero.

2.2.6 The Power ARCH Model

The power ARCH (PARCH) model was introduced by Taylor (1986) and Schwert (1989) and models the standard deviation, rather than the variance. It has been generalized in Ding *et al.* (1993) with the power ARCH specification, as follows

$$y_t = \phi_0 + \sum_{j=1}^{s} \phi_j y_{t-j} + \varepsilon_t$$

$$\varepsilon_t \,|\, \Omega_t \sim D(0, \sigma_t^2)$$

$$\sigma_t^{\varphi} = w + \sum_{j=1}^{q} \beta_j \sigma_{t-j}^{\varphi} + \sum_{i=1}^{p} \alpha_i \left(|\varepsilon_{t-i}| - \gamma_i \varepsilon_{t-i} \right)^{\varphi} \qquad (2.7)$$

where the (positive) power φ parameter of the standard deviation, σ_t, can be estimated, rather than imposed. The γ parameters are imposed to capture asymmetry of up to order r, so that $|\gamma_i| \leq 1$ for $i = 1, ..., r$, $\gamma_i = 0$ for all $i > r$, and $r \leq p$. Of course, as in the previous models, if $\gamma = 0$ the response of volatility to shocks is symmetric.

In this specification, if $\gamma_i = 0$ for all i, equation (2.7) reduces to a symmetric model. Moreover, if $\varphi = 2$ and $\gamma_i = 0$ for all i, equation (2.7) reduces to the standard GARCH specification (2.3).

2.3 The GARCH-in-Mean Model

The basic GARCH framework was extended by Engle *et al.* (1987) to allow the conditional mean, y_t, to depend on the conditional variance, σ_t^2. In this class of model, known as GARCH-in-Mean (or GARCH-M), the conditional mean and conditional variance equations are as follows for an AR(s)-GARCH(q, p) model

$$y_t = \phi_0 + \sum_{j=1}^{s} \phi_j y_{t-j} + \psi \sigma_t^2 + \varepsilon_t; \qquad (2.8)$$

$$\varepsilon_t \,|\, \Omega_t \sim D(0, \sigma_t^2);$$

$$\sigma_t^2 = w + \sum_{j=1}^{q} \beta_j \sigma_{t-j}^2 + \sum_{i=1}^{p} \alpha_i \varepsilon_{t-i}^2.$$

That is, the conditional mean of y_t is a linear function of the conditional variance, σ_t^2, which in turn is a linear function of past squared innovations and past conditional variances. Hence, the GARCH-in-Mean model allows for direct feedback between the conditional variance and the conditional mean.

Other variants of the GARCH-in-Mean model allow the conditional mean, y_t, in equation (2.8) to depend on a function of the conditional variance such as, for example, the conditional standard deviation, σ_t, or the log of the conditional variance, $\ln\left(\sigma_t^2\right)$.

2.4   Estimation

The models discussed in the previous two sections are nonlinear and ordinary least squares cannot be used for estimation. The main reason is that ordinary least squares minimizes the residual sum of squares which depends only on the parameters of the conditional mean equation, and not on the parameters of the conditional variance equation. The models are typically estimated by the method of maximum likelihood which allows joint estimation of the parameters in the mean and variance equations as well as likelihood ratio tests of restrictions of the models.

To implement maximum likelihood estimation, we need to specify the conditional distribution of the error term ε_t. Usually the normal (Gaussian) distribution is assumed and the log-likelihood function is formed to find the values of the parameters that maximize it (given the actual data). For example, in the context of the GARCH-in-Mean model, under the normality assumption for the errors, $\varepsilon_t \,|\Omega_t \sim N(0, \sigma_t^2)$, the conditional log likelihood function takes the form

$$l_t = -\frac{T}{2}\ln\left(2\pi\right) - \frac{1}{2}\sum_{t=1}^{T}\ln\sigma_t^2 - \frac{1}{2}\sum_{t=1}^{T}\frac{\varepsilon_t^2}{\sigma_t^2}.$$

The log likelihood function is then maximized with respect to the vectors of the conditional mean equation parameters, $(\phi_0, \phi_1, \cdots, \phi_s, \delta)$, and the conditional variance equation parameters, $(w, \alpha_1, \cdots, \alpha_p, \beta_1, \cdots, \beta_q)$. This will give estimates for the parameters and their standard errors.

2.5   Fat-Tailed Distributions

In many cases the assumption of conditional normality cannot be maintained; for example, the standardized residuals, $\varepsilon_t^2/\sqrt{\sigma_t^2}$, are not normally distributed, having fatter tails and higher peaks than the standard normal distribution. In those cases it is more appropriate to explore different distributions in an attempt to improve the fit of the model. Two distributions commonly employed when working with ARCH models are the Student's t distribution and the generalized error distribution (GED).

The Student's t distribution is given by

$$f(\varepsilon_t \,|v) = \frac{\Gamma\left[(v+1)/2\right]}{\Gamma\left(v/2\right)\sqrt{\pi\left(v-2\right)}} \left(1 + \frac{\varepsilon_t^2}{v-2}\right)^{-(v+1)/2}$$

where $v > 2$ is the degrees of freedom (controlling the tail behavior) and $\Gamma(\cdot)$ is the usual gamma function. This distribution is normalized to have unit variance and becomes the standard normal distribution when $v \to \infty$. Under the heavy-tailed Student's t distribution for the errors, the conditional log-likelihood function for ε_t takes the form

$$l_t = -\frac{T}{2}\ln\left[\frac{\pi\left(v-2\right)\Gamma\left(v/2\right)^2}{\Gamma\left[(v+1)/2\right]^2}\right] - \frac{1}{2}\sum_{t=1}^{T}\ln\sigma_t^2 - \frac{v+1}{2}\ln\left[1 + \frac{\varepsilon_t^2}{(v-2)\sigma_t^2}\right].$$

The degrees of freedom parameter v can be specified a priori or estimated jointly with the other parameters; see Tsay (2010) for more details.

The GED can also be used. The GED has density function

$$f(x) = \frac{\nu \exp\left[-\frac{1}{2}\left|x/\lambda\right|^{\nu}\right]}{\lambda 2^{(1+1/\nu)}\Gamma\left(1/\nu\right)}$$

where $-\infty < x < \infty$, $0 < \nu \le \infty$, $\Gamma(\cdot)$ is the gamma function, and

$$\lambda = \left[\frac{2^{(-2/\nu)}\Gamma\left(1/\nu\right)}{\Gamma\left(3/\nu\right)}\right]^{1/2}.$$

This distribution reduces to a normal distribution if (the tail-thickness parameter) $\nu = 2$. For $\nu < 2$, the distribution of x has fatter tails than the normal (for example, when $\nu = 1$, x has a double exponential distribution). For $\nu > 2$, the distribution of x has thinner tails than the normal (for example, for $\nu = \infty$, x is uniformly distributed on the interval $\left[-3^{1/2}, 3^{1/2}\right]$. Under a GED for the errors, the conditional log-likelihood function takes the form

$$l_t = -\frac{T}{2}\ln\left(\frac{\Gamma\left(1/\nu\right)^3}{\Gamma\left(3/\nu\right)\left(\nu/2\right)^2}\right) - \frac{1}{2}\sum_{t=1}^{T}\ln\sigma_t^2 - \sum_{t=1}^{T}\left[\frac{\Gamma\left(3/\nu\right)\varepsilon_t^2}{\sigma_t^2\Gamma\left(1/\nu\right)}\right]^{\nu/2}.$$

2.6 Conclusion

I have briefly discussed the basic univariate ARCH models and their variations and described how to estimate these models using the method of maximum likelihood under alternative distributional assumptions. Instead of using volatility measures that are based on the assumption of constant volatility, one can use these models to extract volatility estimates from the data. See Bollerslev *et al.* (1992) and Bollerslev *et al.* (1994) for excellent surveys of these methods and econometric models and Tsay (2010, Chapter 3) for a textbook treatment.

Chapter 3

Multivariate Volatility Models

3.1 Introduction

The univariate volatility models have been generalized to the multivariate case. The multivariate models are similar to the univariate ones, except that they also specify equations of how the conditional covariances and correlations move over time. In addition, it is possible to include a cointegrating parameter in the conditional mean equation, in the case that the variables are cointegrated.

The main problem with the multivariate volatility models is that the covariance matrix has to be positive definite at each data point for the likelihood to be defined. In fact, even if all the variances are positive, if the covariances are out of bounds for even one observation, the likelihood function values will be undefined for a set of parameters. Another problem with the multivariate volatility models is that the number of parameters grows very quickly as we increase the number of variables, meaning that the practical limit is three or four variables in a multivariate volatility model.

Multivariate volatility models can be used to investigate a large number of issues in economics and finance. For example, as Bauwens *et al.* (2006, p. 79) put it,

> "is the volatility of a market leading the volatility of other markets? Is the volatility of an asset transmitted to another asset directly (through its conditional variance) or indirectly (through its conditional covariances)? Does a shock on a market increase the volatility on another market, and by how much? Is the impact the same for negative and positive shocks of the same amplitude?"

In this chapter, I briefly discuss some of the generalizations of the univariate volatility models of the previous chapter as well as some highly restricted parameterizations of the multivariate models. See Bauwens *et al.* (2006) and Silvennoinen and Teräsvirta (2011) for more detailed discussions.

3.2 The VECH Model

Consider a multivariate (n-dimensional) stochastic vector process z_t. We adopt the same approach as in the univariate case by writing the mean equation as

$$z_t = \phi_0 + \sum_{j=1}^{s} \phi_j z_{t-j} + e_t \qquad (3.1)$$

$$e_t | \Omega_{t-1} \sim D\left(0,\, H_t\right)$$

where 0 is the null vector, Ω_{t-1} denotes the available information set in period $t - 1$, and H_t is the $n \times n$ conditional covariance matrix.

The VECH model, initially due to Bollerslev *et al.* (1988), specifies the following equation for H_t

$$vech\left(H_t\right) = C + \sum_{j=1}^{q} B_j\, vech\left(H_{t-j}\right) + \sum_{j=1}^{p} A_j\, vech\left(e_{t-j} e_{t-j}'\right) \qquad (3.2)$$

where $vech(\cdot)$ denotes the column-stacking operator applied to the upper portion of the symmetric matrix. In equation (3.2), C is an $n(n+1)/2 \times 1$ vector and A and B are $n(n+1)/2 \times n(n+1)/2$ parameter matrices. The VECH model is very flexible, but also has a number of disadvantages. One is that the number of parameters in the conditional variance equation (3.2) is very large, $n(n+1)/2 + (p+q)\left[n(n+1)/2\right]^2$, rendering the estimation of the parameters computationally demanding. Furthermore, H_t is positive definite only under rather restrictive conditions.

To appreciate how the VECH model works, consider the bivariate case where

$$z_t = \begin{bmatrix} y_t \\ x_t \end{bmatrix},\; \phi_0 = \begin{bmatrix} \phi_y(0) \\ \phi_x(0) \end{bmatrix},\; e_t = \begin{bmatrix} e_{y,t} \\ e_{x,t} \end{bmatrix},$$

$$\phi_j = \begin{bmatrix} \phi_{11}(j) & \phi_{12}(j) \\ \phi_{21}(j) & \phi_{22}(j) \end{bmatrix},\; \text{and } H_t = \begin{bmatrix} h_{yy,t} & h_{yx,t} \\ h_{xy,t} & h_{xx,t} \end{bmatrix}$$

so that

$$vech\left(H_t\right) = vech\left(\begin{bmatrix} h_{yy,t} & h_{yx,t} \\ h_{yx,t} & h_{xx,t} \end{bmatrix}\right) = \begin{bmatrix} h_{yy,t} \\ h_{yx,t} \\ h_{xx,t} \end{bmatrix}$$

$$vech\left(e_t e_t'\right) = vech\left(\begin{bmatrix} e_{y,t} \\ e_{x,t} \end{bmatrix} \begin{bmatrix} e_{y,t} & e_{x,t} \end{bmatrix}\right)$$

$$= vech\left(\begin{bmatrix} e_{y,t}^2 & e_{y,t} e_{x,t} \\ e_{y,t} e_{x,t} & e_{x,t}^2 \end{bmatrix}\right) = \begin{bmatrix} e_{y,t}^2 \\ e_{y,t} e_{x,t} \\ e_{x,t}^2 \end{bmatrix}$$

and

$$C = \begin{bmatrix} c_1 \\ c_2 \\ c_3 \end{bmatrix}, \ B = \begin{bmatrix} b_{11} & b_{12} & b_{13} \\ b_{21} & b_{22} & b_{23} \\ b_{31} & b_{32} & b_{33} \end{bmatrix} \text{ and } A = \begin{bmatrix} a_{11} & a_{12} & a_{13} \\ a_{21} & a_{22} & a_{23} \\ a_{31} & a_{32} & a_{33} \end{bmatrix}.$$

Setting $s = 1$ in equation (3.1) and $p = q = 1$ in equation (3.2), the VECH model in full is given by

$$\begin{bmatrix} y_t \\ x_t \end{bmatrix} = \begin{bmatrix} \phi_y(0) \\ \phi_x(0) \end{bmatrix} + \begin{bmatrix} \phi_{11}(1) & \phi_{12}(1) \\ \phi_{21}(1) & \phi_{22}(1) \end{bmatrix} \begin{bmatrix} y_{t-1} \\ x_{t-1} \end{bmatrix} + \begin{bmatrix} e_{y,t} \\ e_{x,t} \end{bmatrix}$$

and

$$\begin{bmatrix} h_{yy,t} \\ h_{yx,t} \\ h_{xx,t} \end{bmatrix} = \begin{bmatrix} c_1 \\ c_2 \\ c_3 \end{bmatrix} + \begin{bmatrix} b_{11} & b_{12} & b_{13} \\ b_{21} & b_{22} & b_{23} \\ b_{31} & b_{32} & b_{33} \end{bmatrix} \begin{bmatrix} h_{yy,t-1} \\ h_{yx,t-1} \\ h_{xx,t-1} \end{bmatrix}$$

$$+ \begin{bmatrix} a_{11} & a_{12} & a_{13} \\ a_{21} & a_{22} & a_{23} \\ a_{31} & a_{32} & a_{33} \end{bmatrix} \begin{bmatrix} e_{y,t-1}^2 \\ e_{y,t-1}e_{x,t-1} \\ e_{x,t-1}^2 \end{bmatrix}.$$

Hence the mean equations for y_t and x_t are

$$y_t = \phi_y(0) + \phi_{11}(1)y_{t-1} + \phi_{12}(1)x_{t-1} + e_{y,t}$$
$$x_t = \phi_x(0) + \phi_{21}(1)y_{t-1} + \phi_{22}(1)x_{t-1} + e_{x,t}$$

and the variance equations are

$$h_{yy,t} = c_1 + b_{11}h_{yy,t-1} + b_{12}h_{yx,t-1} + b_{13}h_{xx,t-1}$$
$$+ a_{11}e_{y,t-1}^2 + a_{12}e_{y,t-1}e_{x,t-1} + a_{13}e_{x,t-1}^2$$

$$h_{yx,t} = c_2 + b_{21}h_{yy,t-1} + b_{22}h_{yx,t-1} + b_{23}h_{xx,t-1}$$
$$+ a_{21}e_{y,t-1}^2 + a_{22}e_{y,t-1}e_{x,t-1} + a_{23}e_{x,t-1}^2$$

$$h_{xx,t} = c_3 + b_{31}h_{yy,t-1} + b_{32}h_{yx,t-1} + b_{33}h_{xx,t-1}$$
$$+ a_{31}e_{y,t-1}^2 + a_{32}e_{y,t-1}e_{x,t-1} + a_{33}e_{x,t-1}^2$$

suggesting that every conditional variance and covariance is a function of all lagged conditional variances and covariances as well as of all lagged squared residuals and cross-products of residuals.

Clearly, with $n = 2$ and with $s = 1$ in the conditional mean equation (3.1) and $p = q = 1$ in the conditional variance equation (3.2), the model has a total of 27 parameters to be estimated (6 parameters in the conditional mean equation and 21 parameters in the conditional variance equation).

3.3   The Diagonal VECH Model

Bollerslev *et al.* (1988) also presented a simplified version of the VECH model by assuming that the A and B matrices in (3.2) are diagonal. This diagonal representation of the VECH model, known as the 'diagonal VECH' model, has $(1 + p + q)n(n + 1)/2$ parameters in the conditional variance equation.

In the bivariate case $(n = 2)$, and with $s = 1$ in the conditional mean equation and $p = q = 1$ in the conditional variance equation, the diagonal VECH model written out fully is

$$\begin{bmatrix} y_t \\ x_t \end{bmatrix} = \begin{bmatrix} \phi_y(0) \\ \phi_x(0) \end{bmatrix} + \begin{bmatrix} \phi_{11}(1) & \phi_{12}(1) \\ \phi_{21}(1) & \phi_{22}(1) \end{bmatrix} \begin{bmatrix} y_{t-1} \\ x_{t-1} \end{bmatrix} + \begin{bmatrix} e_{y,t} \\ e_{x,t} \end{bmatrix}$$

and

$$\begin{bmatrix} h_{yy,t} \\ h_{yx,t} \\ h_{xx,t} \end{bmatrix} = \begin{bmatrix} c_1 \\ c_2 \\ c_3 \end{bmatrix} + \begin{bmatrix} b_{11} & 0 & 0 \\ 0 & b_{22} & 0 \\ 0 & 0 & b_{33} \end{bmatrix} \begin{bmatrix} h_{yy,t-1} \\ h_{yx,t-1} \\ h_{xx,t-1} \end{bmatrix}$$

$$+ \begin{bmatrix} a_{11} & 0 & 0 \\ 0 & a_{22} & 0 \\ 0 & 0 & a_{33} \end{bmatrix} \begin{bmatrix} e_{y,t-1}^2 \\ e_{y,t-1}e_{x,t-1} \\ e_{x,t-1}^2 \end{bmatrix}.$$

Hence, the conditional mean equations for y_t and x_t are the same as in the full VECH model

$$y_t = \phi_y(0) + \phi_{11}(1)y_{t-1} + \phi_{12}(1)x_{t-1} + e_{y,t}$$
$$x_t = \phi_x(0) + \phi_{21}(1)y_{t-1} + \phi_{22}(1)x_{t-1} + e_{x,t}$$

but the conditional variance equations are

$$h_{yy,t} = c_1 + b_{11}h_{yy,t-1} + a_{11}e_{y,t-1}^2$$
$$h_{yx,t} = c_2 + b_{22}h_{yx,t-1} + a_{22}e_{y,t-1}e_{x,t-1}$$
$$h_{xx,t} = c_3 + b_{33}h_{xx,t-1} + a_{33}e_{x,t-1}^2.$$

Clearly, the diagonal VECH model is too restrictive as no interaction is allowed between the different conditional variances and covariances. In fact, in this model, each element of the covariance matrix, H_t, depends only on past values of itself and past values of $e_{y,t}e_{x,t}$. In other words, variances depend only on past variances and past own squared residuals and covariances depend only on past covariances and past own cross-products of residuals.

With $n = 2$, $s = 1$ in the conditional mean equation, and $p = q = 1$ in the conditional variance equation, the diagonal VECH model has a total of 15 parameters to be estimated.

3.4   The BEKK Model

A model that is a restricted special case of the VECH model is the Baba, Engle, Kraft, and Kroner (BEKK) model, defined in Engle and Kroner (1995). The BEKK model has the attractive property of having the conditional covariance matrix, H_t, positive definite by construction. It is defined as follows

$$z_t = \phi_0 + \sum_{j=1}^{s} \phi_j z_{t-j} + e_t$$

$$e_t|\,\Omega_{t-1} \sim D\left(0, H_t\right)$$

where 0 is the null vector and Ω_{t-1} denotes the available information set in period $t - 1$ and

$$H_t = C'C + \sum_{j=1}^{q}\sum_{k=1}^{K} B'_{kj} H_{t-j} B_{kj} + \sum_{j=1}^{p}\sum_{k=1}^{K} A'_{kj} e_{t-j} e'_{t-j} A_{kj} \qquad (3.3)$$

where C, A_{kj}, and B_{kj} are $n \times n$ parameter matrices and C is upper triangular, ensuring positive definiteness of the conditional covariance matrix H_t; that is, the decomposition of the constant term into a product of two triangular matrices ensures the positive definiteness of H_t. However, the estimation of the full BEKK model involves heavy computations as the conditional variance equation has $(p+q)Kn^2 + n(n+1)/2$ parameters. Even if we assume that each of the A and B matrices is diagonal, the number of parameters is $(p+q)Kn + n(n+1)/2$, which is large. Moreover, equation (3.3) is not linear in parameters and convergence to the global maximum may be difficult.

In equation (3.3), the summation limit K determines the generality of the process. However, an identification problem arises whenever $K > 1$ and Engle and Kroner (1995) provide conditions that eliminate redundant, observationally equivalent representations. In the case of the first order model (with $p = q = K = 1$), equation (3.3) is written as

$$H_t = C'C + B'H_{t-1}B + A'e_{t-1}e'_{t-1}A \qquad (3.4)$$

and there are $n(5n + 1)/2$ parameters to be estimated in this variance equation.

To appreciate the BEKK model, consider the bivariate case ($n = 2$), with $s = 1$ in the conditional mean equation and $p = q = K = 1$ in the conditional variance equation [or, equivalently a BEKK(1,1,1) specification for the conditional variance], so that the model written out fully is

$$\begin{bmatrix} y_t \\ x_t \end{bmatrix} = \begin{bmatrix} \phi_y(0) \\ \phi_x(0) \end{bmatrix} + \begin{bmatrix} \phi_{11}(1) & \phi_{12}(1) \\ \phi_{21}(1) & \phi_{22}(1) \end{bmatrix} \begin{bmatrix} y_{t-1} \\ x_{t-1} \end{bmatrix} + \begin{bmatrix} e_{y,t} \\ e_{x,t} \end{bmatrix}$$

and

$$\begin{bmatrix} h_{yy,t} & h_{yx,t} \\ h_{xy,t} & h_{xx,t} \end{bmatrix} = \begin{bmatrix} c_{11} & c_{12} \\ 0 & c_{22} \end{bmatrix}' \begin{bmatrix} c_{11} & c_{12} \\ 0 & c_{22} \end{bmatrix}$$

$$+ \begin{bmatrix} b_{11} & b_{12} \\ b_{21} & b_{22} \end{bmatrix}' \begin{bmatrix} h_{yy,t-1} & h_{yx,t-1} \\ h_{xy,t-1} & h_{xx,t-1} \end{bmatrix} \begin{bmatrix} b_{11} & b_{12} \\ b_{21} & b_{22} \end{bmatrix}$$

$$+ \begin{bmatrix} a_{11} & a_{12} \\ a_{21} & a_{22} \end{bmatrix}' \begin{bmatrix} e_{y,t-1}^2 & e_{y,t-1}e_{x,t-1} \\ e_{x,t-1}e_{y,t-1} & e_{x,t-1}^2 \end{bmatrix} \begin{bmatrix} a_{11} & a_{12} \\ a_{21} & a_{22} \end{bmatrix}.$$

Hence the mean equations for y_t and x_t are

$$y_t = \phi_y(0) + \phi_{11}(1)y_{t-1} + \phi_{12}(1)x_{t-1} + e_{y,t}$$
$$x_t = \phi_x(0) + \phi_{21}(1)y_{t-1} + \phi_{22}(1)x_{t-1} + e_{x,t}$$

and the variance equations are

$$h_{yy,t} = c_{11}^2 + b_{11}^2 h_{yy,t-1} + 2b_{11}b_{21}h_{yx,t-1} + b_{21}^2 h_{xx,t-1}$$
$$+ a_{11}^2 e_{y,t-1}^2 + 2a_{11}a_{21}e_{y,t-1}e_{x,t-1} + a_{21}^2 e_{x,t-1}^2$$

$$h_{yx,t} = c_{11}c_{12} + b_{11}b_{12}h_{yy,t-1} + (b_{21}b_{12} + b_{11}b_{22})h_{yx,t-1} + b_{21}b_{22}h_{xx,t-1}$$
$$+ a_{11}a_{12}e_{y,t-1}^2 + (a_{21}a_{12} + a_{11}a_{22})e_{y,t-1}e_{x,t-1} + a_{21}a_{22}e_{x,t-1}^2$$

$$h_{xx,t} = c_{12}^2 + c_{22}^2 + b_{12}^2 h_{yy,t-1} + 2b_{12}b_{22}h_{yx,t-1} + b_{22}^2 h_{xx,t-1}$$
$$+ a_{12}^2 e_{y,t-1}^2 + 2a_{12}a_{22}e_{y,t-1}e_{x,t-1} + a_{22}^2 e_{x,t-1}^2.$$

This model has 17 parameters to be estimated (6 parameters in the conditional mean equation and 11 parameters in the conditional variance equation).

3.5   Restricted Correlation Models

Because of computational difficulties with multivariate volatility models, even in low dimensional systems, Bollerslev (1990) introduced the constant conditional correlation (CCC) model which reduces the number of variance equations by allowing variances and covariances to vary over time but restricting the conditional correlations among the e_t elements to be constant.

Assuming that the $n \times n$ conditional correlation matrix, $\boldsymbol{\rho}_t$ (which is symmetric with unit diagonal elements), is time invariant, then we can write

$$\boldsymbol{H}_t = \boldsymbol{D}_t \boldsymbol{\rho} \boldsymbol{D}_t$$

where $\boldsymbol{D}_t$ is an $n \times n$ diagonal matrix with the conditional standard deviations of the e_t elements along the diagonal, $\boldsymbol{D}_t = diag(\sqrt{h_{11,t}}, \cdots, \sqrt{h_{nn,t}})$. Thus, the time varying covariances in $\boldsymbol{H}_t$ are of the form $h_{ij,t} = \rho_{ij}\sqrt{h_{ii,t}}\sqrt{h_{jj,t}}$.

Assuming a GARCH(1,1) specification, the full CCC model is defined as

$$z_t = \phi_0 + \sum_{j=1}^{s} \phi_j z_{t-j} + e_t$$

$$e_t | \Omega_{t-1} \sim D(0, \boldsymbol{H}_t)$$

with

$$diag\,(\boldsymbol{H}_t) = \boldsymbol{C} + \boldsymbol{B}\,diag\,(\boldsymbol{H}_t) + \boldsymbol{A}\,diag\,\left(\boldsymbol{e}_{t-1}\boldsymbol{e}'_{t-1}\right)$$

where *diag* is the operator that extracts the diagonal of a square matrix. In fact, to further reduce the number of parameters, each of the $\boldsymbol{A}$ and $\boldsymbol{B}$ matrices can be assumed to be diagonal, in which case the model reduces to what is refereed to as the 'diagonal CCC' model, an unrealistic model in many empirical applications with spillover effects in volatility.

For example, a bivariate diagonal CCC model, with $s = 1$ in the conditional mean equation, and a GARCH(1,1) specification for the conditional variance is defined as

$$\begin{bmatrix} y_t \\ x_t \end{bmatrix} = \begin{bmatrix} \phi_y(0) \\ \phi_x(0) \end{bmatrix} + \begin{bmatrix} \phi_{11}(1) & \phi_{12}(1) \\ \phi_{21}(1) & \phi_{22}(1) \end{bmatrix} \begin{bmatrix} y_{t-1} \\ x_{t-1} \end{bmatrix} + \begin{bmatrix} e_{y,t} \\ e_{x,t} \end{bmatrix}$$

and

$$\begin{bmatrix} h_{yy,t} \\ h_{xx,t} \end{bmatrix} = \begin{bmatrix} c_1 \\ c_2 \end{bmatrix} + \begin{bmatrix} b_{11} & 0 \\ 0 & b_{22} \end{bmatrix} \begin{bmatrix} h_{yy,t-1} \\ h_{xx,t-1} \end{bmatrix}$$

$$+ \begin{bmatrix} a_{11} & 0 \\ 0 & a_{22} \end{bmatrix} \begin{bmatrix} e_{y,t-1}^2 \\ e_{x,t-1}^2 \end{bmatrix},$$

implying that the volatilities of the y_t and x_t series are not dynamically related, although they are contemporaneously correlated, since $h_{yx,t} = \rho\sqrt{h_{yy,t}h_{xx,t}}$.

Clearly, this type of model might not be suitable in cases where the correlation coefficient tends to change over time. Several authors have proposed parsimonious models for ρ_t to describe the time-varying correlations. See, for example, Tse and Tsui (2002) and Engle (2002) for dynamic conditional correlation (DCC) models.

3.6 Asymmetry

We can also add asymmetry effects to multivariate volatility models, allowing positive values of the residuals to have a different effect than negative ones. Although several different specifications have been proposed in the literature, here I discuss the asymmetric version of the BEKK model, introduced by Grier *et al.* (2004). It is defined as follows

$$z_t = \phi_0 + \sum_{j=1}^{s} \phi_j z_{t-j} + e_t$$

$$e_t | \, \Omega_{t-1} \sim D\left(0, \, H_t\right)$$

with

$$H_t = C'C + B'H_{t-1}B + A'e_{t-1}e_{t-1}'A + D'u_{t-1}u_{t-1}'D, \qquad (3.5)$$

where C, B, A, and D are $n \times n$ matrices, with C being a triangular matrix to ensure positive definiteness of H. This specification allows past volatilities, H_{t-1}, as well as lagged values of ee' and uu', to show up in estimating current volatilities, where u_t captures potential asymmetric responses.

For example, in the bivariate case, with $z_t = (y_t, x_t)'$, we may capture good news about x_t by a positive x_t equation residual, by defining $u_{x,t} = \max\{e_{x,t}, 0\}$. We also may capture bad news about y_t by defining $u_{y,t} = \min\{e_{y,t}, 0\}$. Assuming $s = 1$ in the mean equation, the full bivariate asymmetric BEKK model is written out fully as

$$\begin{bmatrix} y_t \\ x_t \end{bmatrix} = \begin{bmatrix} \phi_y(0) \\ \phi_x(0) \end{bmatrix} + \begin{bmatrix} \phi_{11}(1) & \phi_{12}(1) \\ \phi_{21}(1) & \phi_{22}(1) \end{bmatrix} \begin{bmatrix} y_{t-1} \\ x_{t-1} \end{bmatrix} + \begin{bmatrix} e_{y,t} \\ e_{x,t} \end{bmatrix}$$

and

$$\begin{bmatrix} h_{yy,t} & h_{yx,t} \\ h_{xy,t} & h_{xx,t} \end{bmatrix} = \begin{bmatrix} c_{11} & c_{12} \\ 0 & c_{22} \end{bmatrix}' \begin{bmatrix} c_{11} & c_{12} \\ 0 & c_{22} \end{bmatrix}$$

$$+ \begin{bmatrix} b_{11} & b_{12} \\ b_{21} & b_{22} \end{bmatrix}' \begin{bmatrix} h_{yy,t-1} & h_{yx,t-1} \\ h_{xy,t-1} & h_{xx,t-1} \end{bmatrix} \begin{bmatrix} b_{11} & b_{12} \\ b_{21} & b_{22} \end{bmatrix}$$

$$+ \begin{bmatrix} a_{11} & a_{12} \\ a_{21} & a_{22} \end{bmatrix}' \begin{bmatrix} e_{y,t-1}^2 & e_{y,t-1}e_{x,t-1} \\ e_{x,t-1}e_{y,t-1} & e_{x,t-1}^2 \end{bmatrix} \begin{bmatrix} a_{11} & a_{12} \\ a_{21} & a_{22} \end{bmatrix}$$

$$+ \begin{bmatrix} d_{11} & d_{21} \\ d_{12} & d_{22} \end{bmatrix} \begin{bmatrix} u_{y,t-1}^2 & u_{y,t-1}u_{x,t-1} \\ u_{x,t-1}u_{y,t-1} & u_{x,t-1}^2 \end{bmatrix} \begin{bmatrix} d_{11} & d_{12} \\ d_{21} & d_{22} \end{bmatrix}.$$

Hence the mean equations for y_t and x_t are

$$y_t = \phi_y(0) + \phi_{11}(1)y_{t-1} + \phi_{12}(1)x_{t-1} + e_{y,t}$$
$$x_t = \phi_x(0) + \phi_{21}(1)y_{t-1} + \phi_{22}(1)x_{t-1} + e_{x,t}$$

and the variance equations are

$$\begin{aligned}
h_{yy,t} &= c_{11}^2 + b_{11}^2 h_{yy,t-1} + 2b_{11}b_{21}h_{yx,t-1} + b_{21}^2 h_{xx,t-1} \\
&+ a_{11}^2 e_{y,t-1}^2 + 2a_{11}a_{21}e_{y,t-1}e_{x,t-1} + a_{21}^2 e_{x,t-1}^2 \\
&+ d_{11}^2 u_{y,t-1}^2 + 2d_{11}d_{21}u_{y,t-1}u_{x,t-1} + d_{21}^2 u_{x,t-1}^2
\end{aligned}$$

$$\begin{aligned}
h_{yx,t} &= c_{11}c_{12} + b_{11}b_{12}h_{yy,t-1} + (b_{21}b_{12} + b_{11}b_{22})h_{yx,t-1} + b_{21}b_{22}h_{xx,t-1} \\
&+ a_{11}a_{12}e_{y,t-1}^2 + (a_{21}a_{12} + a_{11}a_{22})e_{y,t-1}e_{x,t-1} + a_{21}a_{22}e_{x,t-1}^2 \\
&+ d_{11}d_{12}u_{y,t-1}^2 + (d_{21}d_{12} + d_{11}d_{22})u_{y,t-1}u_{x,t-1} + d_{21}d_{22}u_{x,t-1}^2
\end{aligned}$$

$$\begin{aligned}
h_{xx,t} &= c_{12}^2 + c_{22}^2 + b_{12}^2 h_{yy,t-1} + 2b_{12}b_{22}h_{yx,t-1} + b_{22}^2 h_{xx,t-1} \\
&+ a_{12}^2 e_{y,t-1}^2 + 2a_{12}a_{22}e_{y,t-1}e_{x,t-1} + a_{22}^2 e_{x,t-1}^2 \\
&+ d_{12}^2 u_{y,t-1}^2 + 2d_{12}d_{22}u_{y,t-1}u_{x,t-1} + d_{22}^2 u_{x,t-1}^2.
\end{aligned}$$

3.7 The Multivariate GARCH-in-Mean Model

As with the univariate GARCH-in-Mean model, the multivariate GARCH-in-Mean model allows the conditional mean, z_t, to depend on the conditional standard deviation, $\sqrt{H_t}$. Assuming a BEKK(1,1,1) specification for the conditional variance, as in (3.4), the multivariate GARCH-in-Mean BEKK model is defined as follows

$$z_t = \phi_0 + \sum_{j=1}^{s} \phi_j z_{t-j} + \sum_{j=0}^{r} \psi_j \sqrt{H_{t-j}} + e_t \tag{3.6}$$

$$e_t | \Omega_{t-1} \sim D(0, H_t)$$

where ψ is an $n \times n$ parameter matrix and

$$H_t = C'C + B'H_{t-1}B + A'e_{t-1}e_{t-1}'A.$$

Note that in the conditional mean equation (3.6), we use the conditional standard deviation, $\sqrt{H_t}$, instead of the conditional variance, H_t, so that it is in the same units of measurement as the z_t process.

The number of parameters in the conditional mean equation of the multivariate GARCH-in-Mean model is large. To reduce this number, and consequently to reduce the generality, one can impose $r = 0$ in equation (3.6).

3.8   VARMA GARCH-in-Mean Models

We can also use (more general) VARMA, GARCH-in-Mean models as they allow us to capture features of the data generating process in a more parsimonious way without adding a large number of parameters (or lagged variables) in the conditional mean equation. For example, assuming $r = 0$ in equation (3.6) and a BEKK(1,1,1) specification for the conditional variance, as in (3.4), the VARMA, GARCH-in-Mean, BEKK model is defined as follows

$$z_t = \phi_0 + \sum_{j=1}^{s} \phi_j z_{t-j} + \psi \sqrt{H_t} + \sum_{l=1}^{L} \theta_l e_{t-l} + e_t \qquad (3.7)$$

$$e_t | \Omega_{t-1} \sim D(0, H_t)$$

where θ is an $n \times n$ parameter matrix and

$$H_t = C'C + B'H_{t-1}B + A'e_{t-1}e_{t-1}'A.$$

The number of parameters in the conditional mean equation of this VARMA, GARCH-in-Mean, BEKK model can be reduced by imposing $L = 1$ in equation (3.7).

3.9   Estimation

Maximum likelihood estimation of multivariate volatility models is analogous to that of the univariate models. In particular, assuming conditional normality of e_t, and letting θ denote the vector of all the parameters to be estimated, then the sample log likelihood function is of the form

$$l(\theta) = -\frac{nT}{2}\ln(2\pi) - \frac{1}{2}\sum_{t=1}^{T}\ln(|H_t|) - \frac{1}{2}\sum_{t=1}^{T}e_t'H_t^{-1}e_t$$

where $e_t = z_t - \mu_t$ with μ_t modeled using a suitable vector ARMA model. As in the univariate case, the parameters could be estimated by maximizing $l(\theta)$ with respect to θ.

In many applications the multivariate Gaussian innovations might fail to capture the kurtosis of the z_t process. As with the univariate models, to allow for a fat-tailed distribution, the multivariate Student t-distribution might be useful; see Tsay (2010, Chapter 10) for more details. Note that the GED distribution that can be used in maximum likelihood estimation of univariate models, does not generalize to multivariate processes.

3.10 Summary and Conclusions

I have reviewed some multivariate volatility models and highlighted their features. As already noted, these models are increasingly used in applied financial econometrics to study a large number of issues such as, for example, whether the correlations between asset returns change over time, whether they are higher at times of crisis, and whether they are increasing in the long run (perhaps because of the globalization of financial markets).

As noted, estimation of these models is not easy. In particular, the models contain too many parameters to be easily applicable. Also, the log-likelihood function may contain a large number of local maxima, in which case convergence to the global maximum might be very difficult. However, this is an active research area and progress on these (as well as some other) issues will greatly contribute to the theory and practice of multivariate volatility models.

Chapter 4

Oil Price Uncertainty*

---

*This article was originally published in the *Journal of Money, Credit and Banking*, Vol. 42, No. 6, John Elder and Apostolos Serletis, "Oil Price Uncertainty," 1137-1159. Copyright 2010 The Ohio State University. Reprinted with permission. RATS code to replicate the results in this chapter can be found in ESTIMA's web page, at www.estima.com/resources_procs.shtml.

4.1   Introduction

As already noted in Chapter 1, the theories of investment under uncertainty and real options predict that uncertainty about, for example, oil prices will tend to depress current investment. The theoretical foundations for such real options in firm-level investment decisions are developed by Henry (1974), Bernanke (1983), Brennan and Schwartz (1985), Majd and Pindyck (1987), Brennan (1990), Gibson and Schwartz (1990), Triantis and Hodder (1990) and Aguerrevere (2009). Bernanke (1983) argues, in addition, that uncertainty about the return to investment at the firm level may create cyclical fluctuations in aggregate investment. Motivated by this theory, we reinvestigate the empirical relationship between uncertainty about oil prices and investment.

Oil prices may affect economic activity through several different channels, or transmission mechanisms. The real-balances and monetary policy channel posits that oil price increases lead to increases in the overall level of prices, thereby reducing real money balances held by households and firms and ultimately aggregate demand. The income transfer channel emphasizes the transfer of income from oil-importing countries to oil-exporting countries associated with oil price increases. Energy prices may also affect economic activity through their effect on the productivity of labor and capital, as in the real business cycle models of Kim and Loungani (1992), Rotemberg and Woodford (1996), and Finn (2000). A feature of these mechanisms is that the effects of oil price shocks are symmetric — positive price shocks reduce economic growth while negative price shocks produce rapid economic growth.

Several authors have noted that this symmetry is apparently inconsistent with the very slow growth that accompanied the collapse in oil prices in the mid-1980s, as well as the failure of the oil price increases beginning in 2002 to produce a recession more readily. For example, Hooker (1996) argues that the estimated linear relation between oil prices and economic activity has diminished since 1973. Several authors, such as Mork (1989), Lee *et al.* (1995), Hamilton (1996), and Hamilton (2003) find that this apparent weakening is illusory, arguing instead that the true relationship between oil prices and real economic activity is nonlinear, with sustained increases in oil prices having different effects than transitory fluctuations or sustained decreases.

More recently, Edelstein and Kilian (2007, 2009) find little evidence of asymmetry in the response of consumption and investment to oil shocks.

In particular, they find that the prior evidence in favor of asymmetry is the result of failing to disaggregate investment in domestic energy exploration from investment in energy consuming industries and of misidentification associated with an exogenous event during 1986, such as the Tax Reform Act of 1986 (TRA86). Similarly, Edelstein and Kilian (2007) find no evidence of asymmetric responses to oil price shocks.

Mechanisms that could produce an asymmetric relationshipbetween oil prices and economic activity, such as frictions associated with the costly reallocation of specialized labor and capital across economic sectors, are described by Davis (1987) and detailed in a theoretical model by Hamilton (1988). A complementary mechanism that also produces an asymmetric relationship between oil prices and economic activity is detailed in the theories of investment under uncertainty and real options, as in Henry (1974), Bernanke (1983), Brennan and Schwartz (1985), Majd and Pindyck (1987), and Brennan (1990). In these models, uncertainty about the return to investment due to, for example, energy prices may create cyclical fluctuations in investment. The effect arises from the firm's joint decision of which irreversible investments to commit resources to, and when to commit those resources. Uncertainty about the future return on the investment induces optimizing agents to postpone investment as long as the expected value of additional information exceeds the expected short-run return to current investment. As uncertainty is resolved, the propensity of firms to commit investible resources increases. In this sense, the effect of uncertainty on the decision to commit resources is analogous to the effect of uncertainty on the decision to exercise a call option on a dividend-paying financial asset. Increased uncertainty about the return to the underlying financial asset will tend to delay the decision to exercise. Therefore, uncertainty may diminish the willingness of individual firms to commit resources to irreversible investments and, similarly, the willingness of consumers to spend on illiquid durables. This suggests, for example, that uncertainty about oil prices may cause auto manufacturers to delay decisions on whether to commit resources to the development of gas-guzzling SUVs or fuel efficient vehicles, and may cause consumers to delay decisions on which vehicles to purchase.

Bernanke (1983) also argues that such micro-level investment decisions can create macro-level cyclical fluctuations, for two reasons. The first is that the macroeconomy may not be sufficiently diversified from certain large industries, such as automobiles, so as to be immune from industry level fluctuations. The second is that, under imperfect information, agents may be unsure of the permanence of the initial shock to investment, thereby converting a transitory shock into a more persistent disturbance.

Relatively few studies investigate the direct effects of uncertainty about oil prices on the real economy. Pindyck (1991) provides a survey of issues related to uncertainty and suggests that oil price uncertainty may have contributed to the recessions of 1980 and 1982. Ferderer (1996) finds that oil price uncertainty adversely affected output in the United States over the 1970 to 1990 period, while Hooker (1996) reports evidence that this relationship had deteriorated over the 1973-1994 period. Edelstein and Kilian (2007, 2009) find little evidence of asymmetries that would be consistent with an uncertainty effect.

In this chapter, we examine the direct effects of oil price uncertainty on real economic activity, utilizing an empirical model that simultaneously estimates the parameters of interest in an internally consistent fashion. The model is based on a structural VAR that is modified to accommodate GARCH-in-Mean errors, as detailed in Elder (1995, 2004). As a measure of uncertainty about the impending real oil price, we utilize the conditional standard deviation of the forecast error for the change in the real price of oil.

Our principal result is that uncertainty about the price of oil has had a negative and significant effect on real GDP, durables consumption, several components of fixed investment and industrial production over the post-1975 period, even after controlling for lagged oil prices and lagged real output. A graphical analysis shows that our measure of uncertainty about oil prices has been more elevated and variable since the mid-1980s, with spikes during 1986, the recession of 1990-91 and smaller spikes before and after the recession of 2001. Prior to 1985, oil price uncertainty was low relative to the second half of the sample, but with increases prior to the recession of 1981 and during the recession of 1982.

We investigate whether our results may be driven by two issues raised by Edelstein and Kilian (2007) – the aggregation of investment in domestic energy producing with energy consuming industries, and misidentification associated with an exogenous event in 1986 such as TRA86. To investigate the first issue, we estimate the effects of oil price uncertainty on the components of fixed investment that are separate from domestic energy exploration, and find that oil price uncertainty negatively affects durables consumption as well as some, but not all, components of non-residential fixed investment in structures. To investigate the latter issue, we estimate the effects of oil price uncertainty on durables consumption, include dummy variables for 1986, and estimate our model over the post-1986 sample. Our results are largely robust to these modifications.

We also conduct impulse-response analysis. Consistent with much of the literature, our impulse-responses are not estimated very precisely (we report one standard error confidence bands), but we find some evidence that accounting for uncertainty about oil prices tends to alter the estimated response of real output to an oil price shock. In particular, accounting for oil price uncertainty tends to reinforce the decline in real GDP in response to higher oil prices, while moderating the short-run response of real GDP to lower oil prices.[1] The effect of accounting for oil price uncertainty on domestic energy producing industries is more dramatic, with mining-related expenditures falling precipitously in response to lower oil prices, but increasing much less in response to higher oil prices.

There are a few caveats in interpreting our results. First, our model has one component in the conditional mean that is non-linear, so our impulse-response functions may not scale proportionately with the size of the shock. To facilitate interpretation, we compare our impulse-responses to those generated by a more traditional linear model.

Second, our proxy for uncertainty is the conditional variance of oil prices. This proxy reflects the dispersion in the forecast error generated by an econometric model applied to historical data, and may not capture other forward-looking components of uncertainty that are not parameterized in the model. It may also be correlated with some other factor that is driving our result. ARCH based measures of uncertainty, however, have been very common, at least since their seminal application by Engle (1982) to inflation uncertainty.

Third, our model does not decompose innovations in oil prices into components representing demand and supply as in Kilian (2009a). In this sense, our "oil price shocks" may reflect the average composition of oil demand and oil supply shocks over the sample period.

The chapter is organized as follows. Section 4.2 provides a brief description of the empirical model and addresses estimation issues. Section 4.3 presents the data and draws on the large empirical literature dealing with identification issues in structural VARs. Sections 4.4 and 4.5 assess the appropriateness of the econometric methodology by various information criteria, discuss the empirical results, and investigate the robustness of these results. The final section concludes.

---

[1] In this context, higher and lower oil prices refers to positive and negative orthogonalized innovations in the price of oil.

4.2   The Empirical Model

As indicated above, we measure uncertainty about real oil prices as the standard deviation of the one-step-ahead forecast error, conditional on the contemporaneous information set. The standard deviation of this forecast error is a measure of dispersion in the forecast, and as such, is a measure of uncertainty about the impending realization of the price of oil. Such time series measures of uncertainty have been very common, at least since Engle (1982) and Bollerslev (1986) applied univariate ARCH and GARCH models to measure inflation uncertainty.

Our empirical model is a bivariate quarterly model in real GDP growth and the change in the real price of oil and was first developed in Elder (1995, 2004). The operational assumption is that the dynamics of the structural system can be summarized by a linear function of the variables of interest plus a term related to the conditional variance, so that the structural system can be represented as

$$ \boldsymbol{B}\boldsymbol{y}_t = \boldsymbol{C} + \boldsymbol{\Gamma}\boldsymbol{y}_{t-1} + \boldsymbol{\Gamma}_2\boldsymbol{y}_{t-2} + \cdots + \boldsymbol{\Gamma}_p\boldsymbol{y}_{t-p} + \boldsymbol{\Lambda}(L)\boldsymbol{H}_t^{1/2} + \boldsymbol{e}_t \qquad (4.1) $$

where $\dim(\boldsymbol{B}) = \dim(\boldsymbol{\Gamma}_i) = (n \times n)$, $\boldsymbol{e}_t \,|\Omega_{t-1} \sim$ iid $N(\boldsymbol{0}, \boldsymbol{H}_t)$, $\boldsymbol{\Lambda}(L)$ is a matrix polynomial in the lag operator, and Ω_{t-1} denotes the information set at time $t - 1$, which includes variables dated $t - 1$ and earlier. The system is identified by imposing a sufficient number of exclusion restrictions on the matrix $\boldsymbol{B}$, and assuming that the structural disturbances, $\boldsymbol{e}_t$, are uncorrelated.

This specification allows the matrix of conditional standard deviations, denoted $\boldsymbol{H}_t^{1/2}$, to affect the conditional mean. Testing whether oil price volatility affects real economic activity is a test of restrictions on the elements of $\boldsymbol{\Lambda}(L)$ which relate the conditional standard deviation of oil prices, given by the appropriate element of $\boldsymbol{H}_t^{1/2}$, to the conditional mean of $\boldsymbol{y}_t$. That is, if oil price volatility has adversely affected output growth, then we would expect to find a negative and statistically significant coefficient on the conditional standard deviation of oil in the output equation. In our application, the vector $\boldsymbol{y}_t$ includes real output growth and the change in the real price of oil, although we also investigate the robustness of our results to alternative measures of the price of oil and of the level of economic activity, as well as to higher-order dimensions of the model.

The conditional variance $\boldsymbol{H}_t$ is modeled as bivariate GARCH, a general version of which is presented in Bollerslev *et al.* (1988) and Engle and

Kroner (1995) as

$$h_t = C_v + \sum_{j=1}^{J} F_j \, vech \left(e_{t-j} e'_{t-j}\right) + \sum_{i=1}^{I} G_i h_{t-i}$$

$$z_t \sim \text{iidN}(0, I);$$

$$e_t = H_t^{1/2} z_t$$

where C_v is $n^2 \times 1$, F and G are $n^2 \times n^2$, and $h_t = \text{vech}(H_t)$. This specification is too general for most applications, however, with $n(n+1)(n^2+n+1)/2$ distinct variance function parameters for $J = I = 1$. This specification also does not ensure that H_t is positive definite.

Elder (2004) shows that imposing a common identifying assumption in structural VARs greatly simplifies the variance function written in terms of the structural disturbances. That is, given the zero contemporaneous correlation of structural disturbances, the conditional variance matrix H_t is then diagonal, substantially reducing the requisite number of variance functions parameters. Redimensioning the variance function parameter matrices C_v, F, and G, the variance function reduces to

$$diag(H_t) = C_v + \sum_{j=1}^{J} F_j \, diag \left(e_{t-j} e'_{t-j}\right) + \sum_{i=1}^{I} G_i \, diag \left(H_{t-i}\right) \qquad (4.2)$$

where *diag* is the operator that extracts the diagonal from a square matrix. If we impose the additional restriction that the conditional variance of $y_{i,t}$ depends only on its own past squared errors and its own past conditional variances, the parameter matrices F_j and G_i are also diagonal. Given the focus of this chapter, this assumption is not restrictive, and it can be relaxed if we have particular interest in how the lagged volatility of one variable may interact with the conditional variance of another. We therefore estimate the variance function given by equation (4.2), with $J = I = 1$.

The bivariate GARCH-in-Mean VAR, equations (4.1) and (4.2), can be estimated by full information maximum likelihood (FIML), which avoids Pagan's (1984) generated regressor problems associated with estimating the variance function parameters separately from the conditional mean parameters, as in Lee *at al.* (1995). The procedure is to maximize the log likelihood with respect to the structural parameters B, C, Γ_1, $\Gamma_2, \cdots, \Gamma_p$, Λ, C_v, F, and G, where

$$l_t = -(n/2) \ln(2\pi) + \frac{1}{2} \ln |B|^2 - \frac{1}{2} \ln |H_t| - \frac{1}{2} (e_t H_t^{-1} e'_t).$$

We set the pre-sample values of the conditional variance matrix H_0 to their unconditional expectation and condition on the pre-sample values $y_0, y_{t-1}, \cdots, y_{t-p+1}$. To ensure that H_t is positive definite and e_t is covariance stationary, the following restrictions are imposed: C_v is element-wise positive, F and G are element-wise nonnegative, and the eigenvalues of $(F+G)$ are less than one in modulus. Provided that the standard regularity conditions are satisfied, full information maximum likelihood estimates are asymptotically normal and efficient, with the asymptotic covariance matrix given by the inverse of Fisher's information matrix.

This procedure is computationally intensive, as it estimates all the structural parameters simultaneously, unlike the conventional procedures for a homoscedastic VAR. In a homoscedastic VAR, the reduced form parameters are typically estimated by OLS and the structural parameters are recovered in a second stage — either by a Cholesky decomposition or a maximum likelihood procedure applied to the reduced form covariance matrix, requiring numerical optimization over as few as $n(n-1)/2$ free parameters in B. Such simplified estimation schemes are not possible with this model, however, in part because the information matrix is not block diagonal.

Impulse responses are calculated as described in Elder (2003). The Monte Carlo method used to construct the confidence bands is described in Hamilton (1994, p. 337), adopted to our model. That is, the impulse responses are simulated from the maximum likelihood estimates (MLEs) of the model's parameters. Confidence intervals are generated by simulating 1,000 impulses responses, based on parameter values drawn randomly from the sampling distribution of the MLEs, where the covariance matrix of the MLEs is derived from an estimate of Fisher's information matrix.

4.3 Data and Identification

To guide the specification of our model, we draw on the extensive VAR literature that relates oil prices to the real economy, which includes, for example, Hamilton (1983, 1996, 2009), Mork (1989), Lee et al. (1995), Hooker (1996), Bernanke et al. (1997), Hamilton and Herrera (2004), Edelstein and Kilian (2007, 2009), and Kilian (2009a, 2009b).

There is wide variation in these empirical specifications, in terms of the number of variables, measures of output and frequency of the observations. Kilian (2009a) and related papers argue in favor of a bivariate system with quarterly observations on the real price of oil and real GDP growth. Our baseline model is based on this specification, but to ensure that our results are robust to other common specifications, we estimate a bivariate GARCH-in-Mean VAR with several different measures of output and at both quarterly and monthly frequencies.

We measure the price of oil as the composite refiners' acquisition cost (RAC) of crude oil, as compiled by the U.S. Department of Energy. This price index is a weighted average of domestic and imported crude oil costs, including transportation and other fees paid by refiners, and therefore measures the price of crude as an input to production. By including the cost of imported oil, the refiners' acquisition cost of crude oil measures oil prices more broadly than domestic price measures, such as the West Texas Intermediate (WTI) crude oil price at Chicago, which is the price paid to domestic producers in the United States. While only a fraction of the oil traded in the United States is contracted at WTI, the two prices are, at monthly frequencies, very similar.

We obtain a measure of the real price of oil by deflating the refiners' acquisition cost of crude oil by the GDP deflator. We measure output by real GDP. To ensure the robustness of our results, we also utilize the WTI crude oil price and less aggregated measures of output, such as the components of private domestic investment and real personal consumption expenditures on durables. Our pre-sample begins in 1974:2, coinciding with the availability of our oil price series. A detailed description of the data used in this chapter is provided in Appendix Table A1.

We estimate our model using logarithmic first differences of the real price of oil and real GDP, as do Lee *et al.* (1995) and Edelstein and Kilian (2007). We also impose the usual identifying procedure in VARs, which allows us to estimate $n(n-1)/2$ free parameters in B, subject to a rank condition. In a bivariate VAR, we can estimate one free parameter in B. There are different approaches in the literature, but we follow Edelstein and Kilian (2007) and allow the real output growth rate to respond to contemporaneous innovations in the change in the real price of oil.

4.4 Empirical Evidence

We use quarterly data for the bivariate GARCH-in-Mean VAR over the period from 1974:2 to 2008:1. The Schwarz information criterion (SIC) suggests that less than four lags may be sufficient to summarize the dynamics of the system, but we include a full year of lags given the arguments advanced by Hamilton (1996), Hamilton and Herrera (2004), and Edelstein and Kilian (2007). These authors stress that the primary effect of oil prices on real output occurs at or before one year, and so emphasize the importance of including at least one year of lags. Conditioning on four pre-sample observations, our usable sample then begins in 1975:2.

We therefore estimate a bivariate GARCH-in-Mean VAR with four lags, using quarterly observations on the log change in the real price of oil and the log change in real GDP over 1975:2 to 2008:1. To ensure that our specification is consistent with the data, we calculate the Schwarz information criterion for the conventional homoscedastic VAR and our bivariate GARCH-in-Mean VAR. The Schwarz criterion includes a substantive penalty for the additional parameters required to estimate GARCH models, and so an improvement in the Schwarz criterion suggests strong evidence in favor of our specification. The values of the Schwarz criterion reported in Table 4.1 indicate that the bivariate GARCH-in-Mean VAR captures important features of the data, with the Schwarz criterion for the bivariate GARCH-in-Mean VAR being considerably lower than that for the conventional homoscedastic VAR.

Table 4.1 Model Specification Tests

Model and sample	VAR	Bivariate GARCH-M VAR
Real Oil Price (RAC), Real GDP 1975:2-2008:1	2,189	2,159

The point estimates of the variance function parameters of the bivariate GARCH-in-Mean VAR are reported in Table 4.2 and provide further support for the specification. There is evidence of GARCH in real GDP and evidence of ARCH in the real price of oil. At a quarterly frequency, the volatility process for the real price of oil is apparently not very persistent, as only the coefficient on the lagged squared errors is significant.

Table 4.2 Coefficient Estimates for the Variance Function of the
Bivariate GARCH-in-Mean VAR

Equation	Conditional variance	Constant	$e_i^2(t-1)$	$H_{i,i}(t-1)$
Real oil price	$H_{1,1}(t)$	2,066.54**	0.413**	0.00
		(6.32)	(3.38)	
Real GDP	$H_{2,2}(t)$	0.239	0.189**	0.795**
		(0.95)	(2.68)	(8.86)

Notes: These are the parameter estimates for the free elements in $\boldsymbol{F}$ and $\boldsymbol{G}$ from the model given by equations (4.1) and (4.2) with $e_t \sim N(\boldsymbol{0}, \boldsymbol{F}_t)$.
Each row in the table represents an equation from the associated bivariate GARCH-in-Mean VAR. Asymptotic t-statistics are in parentheses.
A coefficient of 0.00 indicates that the nonnegativity constraint is binding.
** Denotes significance at the 5% level.
* Denotes significance at the 10% level.

The primary coefficient of interest relates to the effect of real oil price uncertainty on real GDP. This is the coefficient on the conditional standard deviation of real oil price changes in the output growth equation, which is reported in the first entry of Table 4.3 as −0.022. The null hypothesis that the true value of this coefficient is zero is rejected with a t-statistic of 2.30, thus providing evidence to support the hypothesis that higher oil price uncertainty tends to decrease real economic activity. Hence, uncertainty about the real price of oil has tended to reduce real GDP over our sample and that effect is statistically significant at conventional levels.

To test whether we have unreasonably restricted an additional role for oil price uncertainty in the oil equation, or for output uncertainty in either the oil price equation or the output equation, we have estimated each of these models individually and calculated the SIC. In each case, the SIC deteriorates, with very little improvement in the log likelihood. This suggests that focusing on the effect of oil price uncertainty on output is a reasonable description of the data.

To assess the effect of incorporating oil price uncertainty on the dynamic response of real GDP to an oil price shock, we plot the associated impulse responses in Figure 4.1, simulated from the maximum likelihood estimates of the model's parameters. The impulse responses are based on an oil shock

Oil Price Uncertainty

equal to the annualized unconditional standard deviation of the change in
the real price of oil, which is reported in Appendix Table A1. We choose
a shock of this magnitude to make the impulses comparable to those of
standard homoscedastic VAR. We simulate the response of real output to
both a positive and negative oil price shock, to investigate whether the
responses to positive and negative shocks are symmetric or asymmetric.
We also report one-standard error bands.

Table 4.3 Coefficient Estimates on Oil Volatility

Measure of real output	Coefficient on $\sqrt{H_{1,1}(t)}$
Real GDP	-0.022^{**} (2.30)
Real GDP (1967:1-2008:1) with WTI	-0.011^{**} (2.47)
Real PCE: Durable goods	-0.107^{**} (2.28)
Real gross private investment	-0.153^{**} (2.04)
Real PFI in nonresidential structures:	
- commercial and health care	-0.165^{**} (2.39)
- manufacturing	-0.236 (1.47)
- power and communication	0.022 (0.36)
- mining, exploration, shafts and wells	-0.462^{**} (2.26)
- other	-0.183^{**} (4.02)
Real PFI minus mining, exploration, shafts and wells	-0.048 (1.37)
Real PFI nonresidential equipment and software	-0.038 (1.00)
Industrial production monthly	-0.017^{*} (1.88)

Notes: These are the parameter estimates for the free elements in Λ from the
structural VAR with bivariate GARCH given by equations (4.1) and (4.2), with
$e_t \sim N(\mathbf{0}, \boldsymbol{H}_t)$. $\boldsymbol{H}_t^{1/2}$ denotes the conditional standard deviation of the relevant
measure of oil prices. Absolute t-statistics are in parentheses. The measure of
the real oil price is based on the RAC of crude and the sample is 1975:02-2008:01,
except as indicated.
** Denotes significance at the 5% level.
* Denotes significance at the 10% level.

Consider first the top panel of Figure 4.1, which reports the response
of real output to a positive oil price shock. The impulse response indicates
that, accounting for the effects of oil price uncertainty, an oil price shock
tends to reduce real GDP growth immediately, inducing a downward revi-
sion in the annualized growth rate of real GDP by about 70 basis points

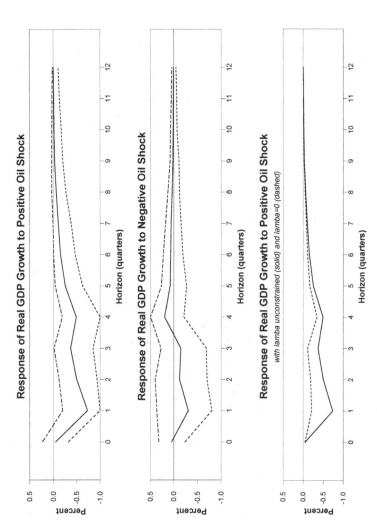

Fig. 4.1 Impulse Responses for Bivariate GARCH-M VAR

after one quarter. The dynamic effect of the positive shock to the real price of oil is also relatively persistent. The estimated precision with which we estimate this effect is consistent with impulse responses over post-1973 samples reported, for example, by Hooker (1996) and Hamilton (1996, Figure 4.3).

In order to quantify the dynamic response of real GDP to oil price shocks, in the second panel of Figure 4.1 we report the impulse response of real GDP to a negative oil price shock. Clearly, our model estimates this effect very imprecisely, as the response of real GDP is well within one standard error of zero at all horizons. Hence, in our model the responses to positive and negative shocks are not symmetric, in that the effect of a positive shock is different from that of a negative shock. Our point estimates indicate that the estimated uncertainty effect is so large as to cause real GDP to decline in response to a negative oil shock. This is not in accordance with standard economic theories, but our estimate of this response is not statistically significant. Such a result is also reported by Lee *et al.* (1995), who find that only the responses to positive shocks are statistically significant while responses to negative shocks are not.

Next, we compare the response of real GDP to a positive oil shock as estimated by our model with that from a model in which oil price uncertainty is restricted from entering the real GDP growth equation — i.e., from a model with the relevant element of Λ (that is, Λ_{21}) constrained to zero. We make such a comparison in the bottom panel of Figure 4.1, where the response of real GDP to a positive oil price shock (from the first panel of Figure 4.1) is repeated as the solid line, with the error bands being suppressed for clarity, and the response of real GDP to a positive oil price shock, when oil uncertainty is restricted from entering the real GDP growth equation, is plotted as the dashed line. That is, the dashed line is constructed by using the parameter estimates from a bivariate GARCH-in-Mean VAR with the coefficient on oil price uncertainty in the real GDP equation, Λ_{21}, restricted to zero.

The solid line in the bottom panel of Figure 4.1 indicates that, when oil price uncertainty is accounted for, the response of real GDP growth to an oil price shock is negative and more pronounced than when oil price uncertainty is excluded from the output equation (dashed line – with $\Lambda_{21} = 0$). That is, the response of real GDP growth to a positive oil price shock is amplified when we allow feedback from the conditional standard deviation of oil price changes to output growth.

In Figure 4.2 we plot the real GDP growth rate, the RAC of crude oil, and the conditional standard deviation of the percentage change in the price of oil over the 1975:2 to 2008:1 sample, with NBER recessions shaded. These plots illustrate the tendency of oil price uncertainty, as parameterized by the bivariate GARCH-in-Mean model, to be high when oil prices exhibit either a large positive or large negative movement. In particular, oil price uncertainty spiked considerably during the 1990-91 recession and rose more modestly around the 2001 recession. Oil price uncertainty was also very high during the mid-1980s, when the price of oil collapsed from over $30 per barrel (in November, 1985) to less than $12 per barrel (in March, 1986). Interestingly, real GDP growth was very low during much of this episode, despite the rapid drop in oil prices. The lack of output growth during this period of dramatically falling oil prices is sometimes attributed to the frictions in the reallocation of labor and capital, as in Davis and Haltiwanger (2001). Our results provide evidence of a complementary mechanism, the effects of heightened uncertainty about impending oil prices.

Pindyck (1991) suggests that oil price uncertainty may have contributed to the recessions of 1980 and 1982, but the third panel of Figure 4.2 indicates that oil price uncertainty was low during this period, at least relative to the period since 1986. Closer inspection, however, reveals increases in oil price uncertainty that are large relative to other years in the 1976:1-1986:1 period. The fourth panel of Figure 4.2 plots oil price uncertainty rescaled for this period. During this period of relative stable oil prices, oil price uncertainty increased from 45% to more than 60% just prior to the 1980 recession, and from 45% to 55% at the start of the 1981 recession. These movements in oil price uncertainty, although dwarfed by the post-1986 period, where unusually large for that time.

More recently, from 2002 through 2008, oil prices have trended upward and oil price uncertainty was erratic, but below previous episodes. In particular, this trend since 2002 did not generate any particularly large spikes in oil price uncertainty. Our empirical results suggest that this is an important feature that may have mitigated the effects of rising oil prices compared to periods of more rapid increases.

Finally, a sense of the economic significance of the effect of oil price uncertainty on real GDP growth can be assessed, to some extent, by examining the estimated effect of oil price uncertainty on real GDP growth for realistic changes in the conditional standard deviation of the change in the real price of oil. Our estimates indicate that the median change in the conditional standard deviation of the (annualized) growth rate in the price of oil is 19.6 percentage points. A 20 percentage point increase in oil

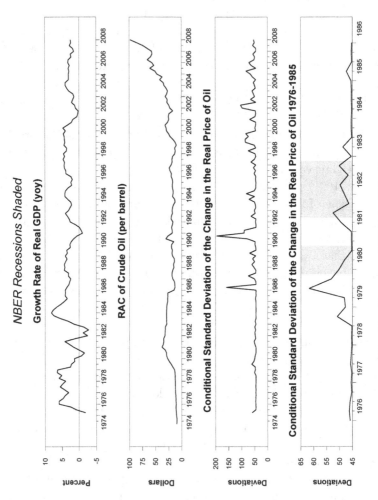

Fig. 4.2 Output and Oil Price Volatility

price uncertainty would, in isolation, suppress the (annualized) quarterly growth rate of real GDP by about $-0.02 \times 20\% = -40$ basis points. It is important to note, however, that this analysis ignores dynamic interactions that would be captured in an impulse-response framework.

4.5 Robustness

Our results thus far suggest that uncertainty about the real price of oil has tended to cause real GDP growth to decline and that the responses to positive and negative shocks are asymmetric. In this section, we investigate the robustness of our results to alternative measures of the oil price and of the level of economic activity. We also evaluate alternative hypotheses in light of concurrent research that has found little evidence of asymmetry.

4.5.1 *Alternative Measures of Oil Prices and Economic Activity*

To investigate robustness, we reestimate the bivariate GARCH-in-Mean VAR using alternative measures of the level of economic activity and the price oil, various sample periods, as well as dummy variables to control for potentially exogenous events as suggested by Edelstein and Kilian (2007). As an alternative measure of the price of oil over an alternative sample, we use the spot price on West Texas Intermediate (WTI) crude oil, deflated by the GDP deflator. Since this oil price series is available over a longer horizon, we estimate our model beginning in 1967:1. As reported in the second entry of Table 4.3, the coefficient on oil price uncertainty is again negative (-0.011) and statistically significant (with a t-statistic of 2.47).

The uncertainty effect detailed by Bernanke (1983) suggests that the effects of oil price uncertainty will be more pronounced on real investment than on broader measures of real output. To investigate this hypothesis we estimate the effect of oil price uncertainty on real aggregate investment and using the RAC of crude oil as the relevant price of oil. The result with real private domestic investment as the output variable is reported in Table 4.3 (see the fifth entry) and the impulse responses are shown in Figure 4.3, in the same fashion as those in Figure 4.1. Consistent with Bernanke's (1983) theory, we find that the effect of oil price uncertainty on investment is negative (-0.153), statistically significant (the absolute t-statistic is 2.04), and larger in magnitude than the effect on real GDP. Moreover, the

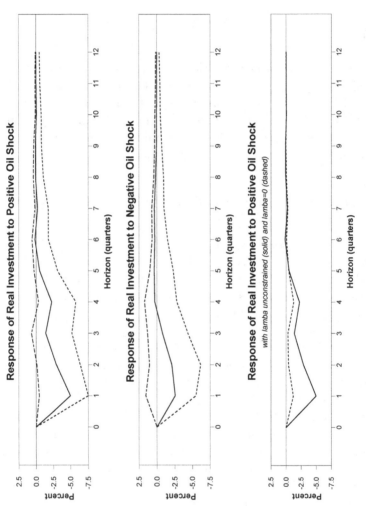

Fig. 4.3   Impulse Responses for Bivariate GARCH-M VAR

dynamic response of real private domestic investment to a positive oil price shock is statistically significant at the 90% level, and asymmetric relative to the response to a negative oil price shock. An apparently anomalous finding is the negative estimated response of real GPDI to a negative oil price shock. This may, however, be due to one component of investment, domestic mining-related expenditures, that drops precipitously in response to negative oil price shocks. We investigate this issue below.

Bernanke (1983) suggests that the effects of oil price uncertainty may affect consumption as well as investment, particularly the consumption of durable goods. We therefore re-estimate our model with real personal consumption expenditures (PCE) on durable goods. Consistent with this hypothesis, we find (see the third entry in Table 4.3) that oil price uncertainty has a negative and significant effect on durables consumption.

4.5.2 The 1986 Tax Reform Act and Investment Aggregation Issues

Edelstein and Kilian (2007, 2009) report evidence that the failure of real GDP to grow rapidly after the sharp drop in oil prices in 1986 was primarily due to declines in private nonresidential investment expenditures, which can be attributed to two factors: (i) provisions in the Tax Reform Act of 1986 such as the repeal of the investment tax credit and the elimination of some real estate tax shelters and (ii) the decline in fixed investment in structures related to mining exploration, shafts, and wells, which is a segment of domestic fixed investment which would naturally fall, rather than increase, in response to lower oil prices. We investigate both these hypotheses below.

We first address Edelstein and Kilian's (2007, 2009) insight related to the sharp decline in fixed investment in structures related to mining exploration, shafts, and wells. They note that a drop in investment in domestic mining equipment, such as that used in energy exploration, is a natural, rather than asymmetric, response to falling world oil prices. They point out that measures of investment which aggregate domestic energy exploration sectors with other sectors may therefore appear to respond asymmetrically to oil shocks, when, in fact, there is no asymmetry. This aggregation issue could clearly be problematic when estimating the response of aggregate investment to rising and falling energy prices, as different components of aggregate investment may move in different directions. This issue, however, may be less problematic when examining the effects of uncertainty about oil prices, since increased uncertainty about oil prices should tend to dampen all forms of investment.

We investigate how uncertainty about the price of oil affects disaggregated measures of private fixed investment (PFI), by focusing on nonresidential investment, as do Edelstein and Kilian (2007). Nonresidential PFI in structures is divided into the following five categories: commercial and health care, manufacturing, power and communication, mining (plus exploration, shafts and wells), and other structures. The other category of nonresidential PFI is equipment and software. The results from fitting the bivariate GARCH-in-Mean VAR to these disaggregated measures of nonresidential PFI are reported in Table 4.3 (see entries 5 to 11).

The point estimate for the coefficient on oil price uncertainty is negative and significant for three of the categories of PFI in nonresidential structures (commercial and health care, mining, and other structures). For the manufacturing component, the coefficient is negative (-0.236), but not significant (with a t-statistic of 1.47). For the third component (power and communication), the coefficient is estimated very imprecisely. Also, taking out mining-related structures from private fixed investment diminishes the precision with which the effect is estimated, as can be seen in entry 10 of Table 4.3. As for PFI in nonresidential equipment and software, the coefficient is negative (-0.038), but statistically insignificant (the t-statistic is 1.00).

The effects of oil price uncertainty are largest in magnitude for mining-related expenditures. This may provide one possible explanation for the large drop in domestic mining-related investment (-45.9%) during 1986, as noted by Edelstein and Kilian (2007). That is, the breakdown in OPEC and subsequent collapse in oil prices contributed to increased uncertainty about future oil prices, such as whether oil prices would continue falling or rebound. In our model, this is captured as an increase in the dispersion of forecasts about future oil prices, or an increase in the conditional standard deviation of oil prices, which then induces firms to be cautious about new irreversible investment decisions. In fact, the third panel of Figure 4.2 indicates that our measure of uncertainty about oil prices was particularly high during 1986.

We argued that the effects of uncertainty about the price of oil are largest on PFI in nonresidential structures related to mining activity, providing additional evidence for the role of uncertainty. As can be seen in Figure 4.4 (which presents impulse response functions in the same fashion as Figures 4.1 and 4.3), the dynamic response of real investment in such structures to negative oil price shocks is also highly significant, with the

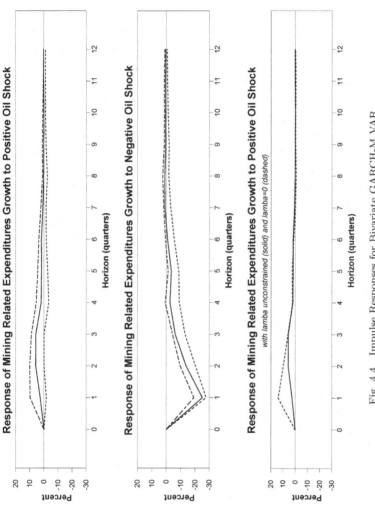

Fig. 4.4 Impulse Responses for Bivariate GARCH-M VAR

direction as shown by Edelstein and Kilian (2007). That is, mining-related investment expenditures drop precipitously after one quarter in response to a negative oil shock. We also find, however, evidence of asymmetry, in that the response of mining-related expenditures to positive oil price shocks is positive, but much smaller in magnitude. Thus, consistent with our impulse-response functions for real GDP and aggregate investment in Figures 4.1 and 4.3, we conclude that accounting for oil price uncertainty tends to exacerbate the response of economic activity to unfavorable oil price shocks, while mitigating the positive response of economic activity to favorable oil price shocks.

We next investigate whether our results regarding the effects of oil price uncertainty are inadvertently due to ignoring possible effects associated with the Tax Reform Act of 1986. Oil prices collapsed in the mid-1980s, at about the same time that the Tax Reform Act of 1986 was enacted. TRA86 contained provisions that had opposing effects on investment in structures that may have affected the decline in aggregate investment during this period, as detailed in the *Survey of Current Business* (January 1987, p. 4). For example, during 1986 non-residential investment in structures declined by 15.5% (continuously compounded) while investment in equipment and software increased by 1.51%. The relevant provisions of TRA86 included: the repeal of the investment tax credit that increased the effective cost of producers' durable equipment, so that businesses had an incentive to substitute some investment in structures for investment in producers' durable equipment; changes in depreciation schedules that provided an incentive for businesses to shift some purchases of some assets, such as autos and structures, from 1987 to 1986; and a reduction in corporate income tax rates that would tend to promote all investment. TRA86 was signed into law during the fourth quarter of 1986 (October), and some of the provisions became effective retroactively on January 1, 1986. There had been considerable debate as to the effective date of various provisions, however, as both the Senate and the House passed resolutions requesting that the effective date for all provisions be postponed to January 1, 1987.

The timing of TRA86 should not affect our identification of the effects of oil price uncertainty on durables consumption, as the primary provisions of TRA86 did not target durables consumption. To investigate whether our estimates of the effects of oil price uncertainty on investment are driven by some exogenous event in 1986 we do the following: (i) we estimate our bivariate GARCH-in-Mean VAR with dummy variables in the output equation for each quarter of 1986; and (ii) we estimate our bivariate GARCH-in-Mean VAR using data from 1987 onward.

As reported in Table 4.4 (which reports results in the same fashion as Table 4.3), including quarterly dummy variables for 1986 has modest effect on our estimates related to real GDP and aggregate investment. The effect of oil price uncertainty on real GDP is negative, but only marginally significant, and the effect on aggregate investment is again negative (-0.172) and significant (with a t-statistic of 1.94). Somewhat surprisingly, the effect of

Table 4.4 Coefficient Estimates on Oil Volatility

	Coefficient on $\sqrt{H_{1,1}(t)}$	
	oil volatility	
Measure of real output	1986 dummies	post-1986
Real GDP	-0.021* (1.73)	-0.002 (1.28)
Real GDP (1967:1-2008:1) with WTI	-0.010** (2.24)	
Real PCE: durable goods	-0.087** (1.54)	-0.145** (2.66)
Real gross private investment	-0.172* (1.94)	-0.057 (0.74)
Real PFI in nonresidential structures:		
- commercial and health care	-0.146** (2.70)	-0.165** (2.41)
- manufacturing	-0.249* (1.75)	-0.196 (1.41)
- power and communication	-0.026 (0.27)	0.038 (0.51)
- mining, exploration, shafts and wells	-0.171 (1.06)	-0.123 (0.96)
- other	-0.221** (4.00)	-0.260** (5.59)
Real PFI minus mining, exploration, shafts and wells	-0.060 (1.44)	-0.035 (1.13)
Real PFI nonresidential equipment and software	-0.039 (0.37)	-0.072 (1.14)
Industrial production monthly	-0.015 (1.54)	-0.055** (2.13)

Notes: These are the parameter estimates for the free elements in Λ from the structural VAR with bivariate GARCH given by equations (4.1) and (4.2), with $e_t \sim N(\mathbf{0}, \mathbf{H}_t)$. $\mathbf{H}_t^{1/2}$ denotes the conditional standard deviation of the relevant measure of oil prices. Absolute t-statistics are in parentheses. In the first column the sample is 1975:02-2008:01, except as indicated, with quarterly and/or monthly dummies for each period in 1986. In the second column the sample is 1987:01-2008:01.
** Denotes significance at the 5% level.
* Denotes significance at the 10% level.

oil price uncertainty on real personal consumption expenditures of durable goods is no longer significant in the presence of quarterly dummy variables for 1986. This loss of significance is probably not attributable to TRA86, however, as we have no reason to believe that TRA86 had a large effect on such expenditures during this time. Regarding the disaggregated measures of investment, for two of the five measures of nonresidential investment in structures (commercial and health care and other structures), the effect of oil price uncertainty is negative and significant at the 5% level. For one measure (manufacturing structures), the effect is negative and significant at the 10% level. Interestingly, the effect of oil price uncertainty on domestic mining-related structures is negative, but not statistically significant. Similarly, the effect on private fixed investment less mining-related structures is negative, but not significant.

Perhaps the most convincing method to control for any effects associated with TRA86 is to reestimate our model over the 1987:1-2008:1 sample period. The sample excludes the spike in oil price uncertainty corresponding to the collapse in oil prices during the first half of 1986, so that any effects of TRA86 cannot be misattributed to this increase in oil price uncertainty. The only caveat is that, given our smaller sample, we might expect some loss of power in our statistical tests.

The results from this subsample are reported in the last column of Table 4.4. Our results are surprisingly robust. The coefficient on oil price uncertainty is again negative and significant on real GDP, durables consumption, aggregate investment and nonresidential investment in commercial and health care structures and other structures.

We consider two additional tests of the robustness of our results. The first is based on higher frequency data with output measured by industrial production. Industrial production is a much narrower measure of economic activity than real GDP, but is a common measure of output available at the monthly frequency. The results for this specification are also reported in Tables 4.3 and 4.4 (see entry 12). The coefficient on oil price uncertainty is reported in Table 4.3 as −0.017 and is significant at the 10% level with a t-statistic of 1.88. Including quarterly dummies for 1986 causes the effect to be estimated less precisely, but over the post-1986 subsample, the effect of oil price uncertainty is again negative (-0.055) and significant (with a t-statistic of 2.13). This result is consistent with our earlier findings regarding the effect of oil price uncertainty on the level of economic activity, and provides further evidence that our results are not driven by one particular specification.

Table 4.5 SIC for Two Models

Measure of real output	VAR with 1986 dummy	MGARCH-M VAR
Real GDP	2,207	2,159*
Real GDP (1967:1-2008:1) with WTI	2,734	2,610*
Real PCE: Durable goods	2,564	2,543*
Real gross private investment	2,634	2,611*
Real PFI in nonresidential structures:		
- commercial and health care	2,781	2,603*
- manufacturing	2,785	2,772*
- power and communication	2,665	2,657*
- mining, exploration, shafts and wells	2,820*	2,826
- other	2,677	2,652*
Real PFI minus mining, exploration, shafts and wells	2,456	2,445*
Real PFI nonresidential equipment and software	2,495	2,484*
Industrial production monthly	7,499	7,281*

Notes: These are the SIC for a linear bivariate VAR with a dummy variable for each period (quarter or month) of 1986 in the output equation and for a bivariate GARCH-M VAR with no dummy variable, except as indicated. The measure of the real oil price is based on the refiner's acquisition cost of crude, except where indicated.
* Denotes the lower of the two SIC values.

Finally, Table 4.5 reports SIC values for a homoscedastic VAR with quarterly dummies and for the bivariate GARCH-in-Mean VAR. Comparisons of the reported SIC values suggest that for all but one specification, the bivariate GARCH-in-Mean VAR is the preferred specification, thereby providing additional support for the bivariate GARCH-M VAR specification.

4.6 Conclusion

The theories of investment under uncertainty and real options predict that uncertainty about, for example, oil prices will tend to depress current investment and consumption. In this chapter, we examine the effects of oil price uncertainty on real economic activity in the United States, in the context of a dynamic bivariate framework in which a structural vector autoregression has been modified to accommodate bivariate GARCH-in-Mean errors, as in Elder (1995, 2004). In this model, oil price uncertainty is the conditional standard deviation of the one-period ahead forecast error of the change in the price of oil. On the basis of information criteria, we find that the bivariate GARCH-in-Mean VAR embodies a better description of the data and is preferred over a homoscedastic VAR.

Our main empirical result is that uncertainty about the price of oil has had a negative and significant effect on real output. The negative and significant effect of oil price uncertainty is robust to several alternative specifications, alternative measures of the price of oil, alternative sample periods and disaggregated measures of output. We also find some evidence that accounting for oil price uncertainty tends to exacerbate the negative dynamic response of real output to a positive oil shock, while dampening the dynamic response of real output to a negative oil price shock. Some of the impulse-response functions, however, are not estimated very precisely. We also find some evidence that the effect of oil price uncertainty is most pronounced on measures of durables consumption and fixed investment, particularly some components of nonresidential fixed investment in structures.

We also investigate whether our results may be driven by issues raised by Edelstein and Kilian (2007): (i) the Tax Reform Act of 1986, they argue caused a large exogenous decline in investment spending during a period of falling oil prices, and (ii) the aggregation of investment spending that includes investment in domestic energy exploration, which naturally falls, rather than increases, in response to falling oil prices. To investigate whether our results are due to misidentification associated with TRA86, we estimated our model with dummy variables for 1986 and over the post-1986 sample. We find that our results are generally robust to one, or both, of these specifications.

To investigate the latter issue, we estimate our model with disaggregated measures of investments. We find that oil price uncertainty significantly affects several measures of nonresidential investment in structures, including mining expenditures. Impulse-response analysis indicates that, when we account for oil price uncertainty, domestic mining expenditures fall precipitously in response to lower oil prices, while mining-related expenditures increase much less dramatically in response to higher oil prices.

Further research might investigate whether our measure of oil price uncertainty might be a proxy for precautionary demand shocks as defined in Kilian (2009a).

Finally, a descriptive analysis shows that uncertainty about the price of oil remained relatively low from 2002 through 2008, despite a steady increase in the price of oil. Our results provide some additional evidence that uncertainty about oil prices may help explain two features of the relationship between oil prices and output — the failure of the dramatic drop in oil prices during the mid 1980s to produce rapid output growth, and the failure of the oil price increases from 2002 through 2008 to induce a recession more readily.

Appendix Table A1. Data Description

Series	Transformation and Frequency	Sample Mean (Std. dev.) Annualized	Description
Real GDP	$400 \times \ln\left(\dfrac{RGDP_t}{RGDP_{t-1}}\right)$ Quarterly	2.92% (3.11%)	Real gross domestic product, seasonally adjusted.
Real PCE on Durables	$400 \times \ln\left(\dfrac{RPCE_t}{RPCE_{t-1}}\right)$ Quarterly	5.06% (12.38%)	Real personal consumption expenditures on Durables, seasonally adjusted.
Real PFI on Mining	$400 \times \ln\left(\dfrac{RPFI_t}{RPFI_{t-1}}\right)$ Quarterly	3.04% (36.71%)	Real PFI, non-residential structures, mining exploration shafts and wells.
Real PFI minus Mining	$400 \times \ln\left(\dfrac{RGPDI_t}{RGPDI_{t-1}}\right)$ Quarterly	3.38% (9.50%)	Real PFI minus Mining-related structures, seasonally adjusted.
Real Oil RAC	$400 \times \ln\left(\dfrac{RAC_t}{RAC_{t-1}}\right)$ Quarterly	7.12% (56.79%)	U.S. refiner acquisition cost of crude oil (composite), deflated by chained GDP deflator
IPI	$1200 \times \ln\left(\dfrac{IPI_t}{IPI_{t-1}}\right)$ Monthly	2.67% (7.75%)	Industrial production index, seasonally adjusted.

Chapter 5

The Asymmetric Effects of Oil Price Shocks*

*This article was originally published in *Macroeconomic Dynamics*, Vol. 15 (Supplement 3), Sajjadur Rahman and Apostolos Serletis, "The Asymmetric Effects of Oil Price Shocks," 437-471. Copyright 2011 Cambridge University Press. Reprinted with permission.

5.1   Introduction

In Chapter 4, we examined the direct effects of oil price uncertainty on real economic activity in the United States, over the modern OPEC period, in the context of a structural VAR that is modified to accommodate GARCH-in-Mean errors, as detailed in Engle and Kroner (1995) and Elder (2004). As a measure of uncertainty about the impending oil price, we used the conditional standard deviation of the forecast error for the change in the price of oil. Their main result is that uncertainty about the price of oil has had a negative and significant effect on real economic activity over the post 1975 period, even after controlling for lagged oil prices and lagged real output. Their estimated effect is robust to a number of different specifications, including alternative measures of the price of oil and of economic activity, as well as alternative sample periods. We also find that accounting for oil price uncertainty tends to reinforce the decline in real GDP in response to higher oil prices, while moderating the short run response of real GDP to lower oil prices.

In this chapter we move the empirical literature forward, by investigating the asymmetric effects of uncertainty on output growth and oil price changes as well as the response of uncertainty about output growth and oil price changes to shocks. In doing so, we use an extremely general bivariate framework in which a vector autoregression is modified to accommodate GARCH-in-Mean errors, as detailed in Engle and Kroner (1995), Grier et al (2004), and Shields et al. (2005). The model allows for the possibilities of spillovers and asymmetries in the variance-covariance structure for real activity and the real price of oil. As in Chapter 4, our measure of oil price change volatility is the conditional variance of the oil price change forecast error. We isolate the effects of oil price change volatility and its asymmetry on output growth and, following Koop et al. (1996), Grier et al (2004), and Hafner and Herwartz (2006), we employ simulation methods to calculate Generalized Impulse Response Functions (GIRFs) and Volatility Impulse Response Functions (VIRFs) to trace the effects of independent shocks on the conditional means and the conditional variances, respectively, of the variables.

We find that our bivariate, GARCH-in-mean, asymmetric VAR-BEKK model embodies a reasonable description of the monthly U.S. data, over the period from 1980:1 to 2010:7. We present evidence that increased uncertainty about the change in the real price of oil is associated with a lower average growth rate of real economic activity. Generalized impulse response experiments highlight the asymmetric effects of positive and negative shocks in the change in the real price of oil to output growth. Also, volatility impulse response experiments reveal that the effect of good news (negative shocks to the change in the real price of oil) on the conditional variance of the change in the real price of oil differs in magnitude and persistence from that of bad news of similar magnitude. This result suggests that, given the relationship between oil price volatility and output, the asymmetric response of oil price volatility to oil price shocks might be a contributing factor in explaining the asymmetric relationship between oil prices and economic activity.

The chapter is organized as follows. Section 5.2 presents the data and Section 5.3 provides a brief description of the bivariate, GARCH-in-Mean, asymmetric VAR-BEKK model. Sections 5.4, 5.5, and 5.6 assess the appropriateness of the econometric methodology by various information criteria and present and discuss the empirical results. The final section concludes the chapter.

5.2 The Data

We use monthly data for the United States, from the Federal Reserve Economic Database (FRED) maintained by the Federal Reserve Bank of St. Louis, over the period from 1980:1 to 2010:7, on two variables — the industrial production index (y_t) and the real price of oil (oil_t). In particular, we use the spot price on West Texas Intermediate (WTI) crude oil as the nominal price of oil and divide it by the consumer price index (CPI) to obtain the real price of oil. Following Bernanke *et al.* (1997), Lee and Ni (2002), and Hamilton and Herrera (2004), we use the industrial production index as a proxy variable for real output. It is to be noted that industrial output reflects only manufacturing, mining, and utilities, and represents only about 20% of total output. The industrial production index, however, captures economic activity that is likely to be directly affected by oil prices and uncertainty about oil prices.

Table 5.1 presents summary statistics for the annualized logarithmic first differences of y_t and oil_t, denoted as $\Delta \ln y_t$ and $\Delta \ln oil_t$, and Figures 5.1 and 5.2 plot the $\ln y_t$ and $\Delta \ln y_t$ and $\ln oil_t$ and $\Delta \ln oil_t$ series, respectively, with shaded areas indicating NBER recessions. Both $\Delta \ln y_t$ and $\Delta \ln oil_t$ are skewed and there is significant amount of excess kurtosis present in the data. Moreover, a Jarque-Bera (1980) test for normality,

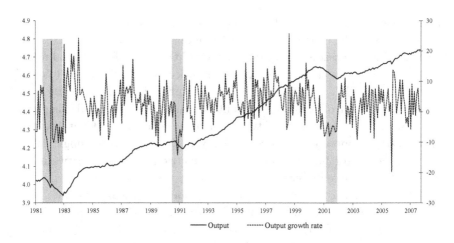

Fig. 5.1   Logged Real Output and the Real Output Growth Rate

distributed as a $\chi^2(2)$ under the null hypothesis of normality, suggests that each of $\Delta \ln y_t$ and $\Delta \ln oil_t$ fails to satisfy the null hypothesis of the test.

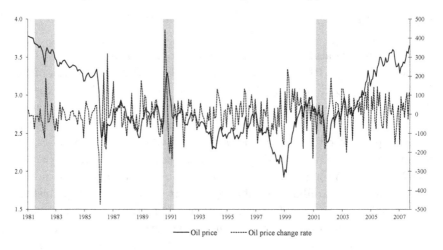

Fig. 5.2   Logged Real Oil Price and the Rate of Change in the Real Price of Oil

A battery of unit root and stationarity tests are conducted in Table 5.1 in $\Delta \ln y_t$ and $\Delta \ln oil_t$. In particular, we report the augmented Dickey-Fuller (ADF) test [see Dickey and Fuller (1981)] and, given that unit root tests have low power against relevant trend stationary alternatives, we also present Kwiatkowski et al. (1992) tests, known as KPSS tests, for level and trend stationarity. As can be seen, the null hypothesis of a unit root can be rejected at conventional significance levels. Moreover, the t-statistics $\widehat{\eta}_\mu$ and $\widehat{\eta}_\tau$ that test the null hypotheses of level and trend stationarity are small relative to their 5% critical values of 0.463 and 0.146 (respectively), given in Kwiatkowski *et al.* (1992). We thus conclude that $\Delta \ln y_t$ and $\Delta \ln oil_t$ are stationary [integrated of order zero, or I(0), in the terminology of Engle and Granger (1987)].

In panel C of Table 5.1, we conduct Ljung-Box (1979) tests for serial correlation in $\Delta \ln y_t$ and $\Delta \ln oil_t$. The Q-statistics, $Q(4)$ and $Q(12)$, are asymptotically distributed as $\chi^2(36)$ on the null hypothesis of no autocorrelation. Clearly, there is significant serial dependence in the data. We also present (in the last column of panel C) Engle's (1982) ARCH χ^2 test statistic, distributed as a $\chi^2(1)$ on the null of no ARCH. The test indicates that there is strong evidence of conditional heteroscedasticity in each of the $\Delta \ln y_t$ and $\Delta \ln oil_t$ series.

Finally, as we are interested in the asymmetry of the volatility response to news, in panel D of Table 5.1 we present Engle and Ng (1993) tests for 'sign bias,' 'negative size bias,' and 'positive size bias,' based on the following regression equations, respectively,

$$\widehat{\varepsilon}_t^2 = \phi_0 + \phi_1 D_{t-1}^- + \xi_t \tag{5.1}$$

$$\widehat{\varepsilon}_t^2 = \phi_0 + \phi_1 D_{t-1}^- \widehat{\varepsilon}_{t-1} + \xi_t \tag{5.2}$$

$$\widehat{\varepsilon}_t^2 = \phi_0 + \phi_1 D_{t-1}^+ \widehat{\varepsilon}_{t-1} + \xi_t \tag{5.3}$$

where $\widehat{\varepsilon}_t$ is the residual from a fourth-order autoregression of the raw data ($\Delta \ln y_t$ or $\Delta \ln oil_t$), treated as a collective measure of news at time t, D_{t-1}^- is a dummy variable that takes a value of one when $\widehat{\varepsilon}_{t-1}$ is negative (bad news) and zero otherwise, $D_{t-1}^+ = 1 - D_{t-1}^-$, picking up the observations with positive innovations (good news), and ϕ_0 and ϕ_1 are parameters. The t-ratio of the ϕ_1 coefficient in each of regression equations (5.1)-(5.3) is defined as the test statistic.

The sign bias test in equation (5.1) examines the impact that positive and negative shocks have on volatility which is not predicted by the volatility model under consideration. In particular, if the response of volatility to shocks is asymmetric (that is, positive and negative shocks to $\widehat{\varepsilon}_{t-1}$ impact differently upon the conditional variance, $\widehat{\varepsilon}_t^2$), then ϕ_1 will be statistically significant. Irrespective of whether the response of volatility to shocks is symmetric or asymmetric, the size (or magnitude) of the shock could also affect volatility. The negative size bias test in equation (5.2) focuses on the asymmetric effects of negative shocks (that is, whether small and large negative shocks to $\widehat{\varepsilon}_{t-1}$ impact differently upon the conditional variance, $\widehat{\varepsilon}_t^2$). In this case, D_{t-1}^- is used as a slope dummy variable in equation (5.2) and negative size bias is present if ϕ_1 is statistically significant. The positive size bias test in equation (5.3) focuses on the different effects that large and small positive shocks have on volatility, and positive size bias is present if ϕ_1 is statistically significant in (5.3). We also conduct a joint test for both sign and size bias using the following regression equation,

$$\widehat{\varepsilon}_t^2 = \phi_0 + \phi_1 D_{t-1}^- + \phi_2 D_{t-1}^- \widehat{\varepsilon}_{t-1} + \phi_3 D_{t-1}^+ \widehat{\varepsilon}_{t-1} + \xi_t. \qquad (5.4)$$

In the joint test in equation (5.4), the test statistic is equal to $T \times R^2$ (where R^2 is the R-squared from the regression) and follows a χ^2 distribution with three degrees of freedom under the null hypothesis of no asymmetric effects.

As can be seen in panel D of Table 5.1, the conditional volatility of output growth is sensitive to the sign and size of the innovation. In particular, there is strong evidence of sign and negative size bias in the output growth volatility, and the joint test for both sign and size bias is highly significant. Also, the conditional volatility of the change in the price of oil displays negative size bias and the joint test for both sign and size bias is significant at conventional significance levels.

5.3   Econometric Methodology

Given the evidence of conditional heteroscedasticity in the $\Delta \ln y_t$ and $\Delta \ln oil_t$ series, we characterize the joint data generating process underlying $\Delta \ln y_t$ and $\Delta \ln oil_t$ as a bivariate GARCH-in-Mean model, as follows

$$\boldsymbol{y}_t = \mathbf{a} + \sum_{i=1}^{p} \boldsymbol{\Gamma}_i \boldsymbol{y}_{t-i} + \sum_{j=0}^{q} \boldsymbol{\Psi}_j \sqrt{h_{t-j}} + \mathbf{e}_t \qquad (5.5)$$

$$\mathbf{e}_t | \Omega_{t-1} \sim (\mathbf{0}, \boldsymbol{H}_t), \qquad \boldsymbol{H}_t = \begin{bmatrix} h_{\Delta \ln y \Delta \ln y, t} & h_{\Delta \ln y \Delta \ln oil, t} \\ h_{\Delta \ln oil \Delta \ln y, t} & h_{\Delta \ln oil \Delta \ln oil, t} \end{bmatrix}$$

where $\mathbf{0}$ is the null vector, Ω_{t-1} denotes the available information set in period $t-1$, and

$$
y_t = \begin{bmatrix} \Delta \ln y_t \\ \Delta \ln oil_t \end{bmatrix} ; e_t = \begin{bmatrix} e_{\Delta \ln y,t} \\ e_{\Delta \ln oil,t} \end{bmatrix} ; h_t = \begin{bmatrix} h_{\Delta \ln y \Delta \ln y,t} \\ h_{\Delta \ln oil \Delta \ln oil,t} \end{bmatrix} ;
$$

$$
a = \begin{bmatrix} a_{\Delta \ln y} \\ a_{\Delta \ln oil} \end{bmatrix} ; \Gamma_i = \begin{bmatrix} \gamma_{11}^{(i)} & \gamma_{12}^{(i)} \\ \gamma_{21}^{(i)} & \gamma_{22}^{(i)} \end{bmatrix} ; \Psi_j = \begin{bmatrix} \psi_{11}^{(j)} & \psi_{12}^{(j)} \\ \psi_{21}^{(j)} & \psi_{22}^{(j)} \end{bmatrix} .
$$

Notice that we have not added any error correction term in the model as the null hypothesis of no cointegration between output ($\ln y_t$) and the real price of oil ($\ln oil_t$) cannot be rejected.

Multivariate GARCH models require that we specify volatilities of $\Delta \ln y_t$ and $\Delta \ln oil_t$, measured by conditional variances. Several different specifications have been proposed in the literature, including the VECH model of Bollerslev *et al.* (1988), the CCORR model of Bollerslev (1990), the FARCH specification of Engle *et al.* (1990), the BEKK model proposed by Engle and Kroner (1995), and the DCC model of Engle (2002). However, none of these specifications is capable of capturing the asymmetry of the volatility response to news.

In this regard, given the asymmetric effects of news on volatility in the $\Delta \ln y_t$ and $\Delta \ln oil_t$ series, we use an asymmetric version of the BEKK model, introduced by Grier *et al.* (2004), as follows

$$
H_t = C'C + \sum_{j=1}^{f} B_j' H_{t-j} B_j
$$

$$
+ \sum_{k=1}^{g} A_k' e_{t-k} e_{t-k}' A_k + D' u_{t-1} u_{t-1}' D \tag{5.6}
$$

where C, B_j, A_k, and D are 2×2 matrices (for all values of j and k), with C being a triangular matrix to ensure positive definiteness of H. In equation (5.6), $u_t = (u_{\Delta \ln y,t}, u_{\Delta \ln oil,t})'$ and captures potential asymmetric responses. In particular, if the change in the price of oil, $\Delta \ln oil_t$, is higher than expected, we take that to be bad news. We therefore capture bad news about oil price changes by a positive oil price change residual, by defining $u_{\Delta \ln oil,t} = \max \{e_{\Delta \ln oil,t}, 0\}$. We also capture bad news about output growth by defining $u_{\Delta \ln y,t} = \min \{e_{\Delta \ln y,t}, 0\}$. Hence, $u_t = (u_{\Delta \ln y,t}, u_{\Delta \ln oil,t})' = (\min \{e_{\Delta \ln y,t}, 0\}, \max \{e_{\Delta \ln oil,t}, 0\})'$.

The specification in equation (5.6) allows past volatilities, H_{t-j}, as well as lagged values of ee' and uu', to show up in estimating current volatilities of $\Delta \ln y_t$ and $\Delta \ln oil_t$. Moreover, the introduction of the uu' term in (5.6) extends the BEKK model by relaxing the assumption of symmetry, thereby allowing for different relative responses to positive and negative shocks in the conditional variance-covariance matrix, H.

There are $n + n^2 (p + q) + n(n+1)/2 + n^2(f + g + 1)$ parameters in (5.5)-(5.6) and in order to deal with estimation problems in the large parameter space we assume that $f = g = 1$ in equation (5.6), consistent with recent empirical evidence regarding the superiority of GARCH(1,1) models — see, for example, Hansen and Lunde (2005). It is also to be noted that we have not included an interest rate variable in the model (in the y_t equation), although it would seem to be important as oil prices affect output through an indirect effect on the rate of interest. We have kept the dimension of the model low because of computational and degree of freedom problems in the large parameter space. For example, with $n = 2$, $p = q = 2$ in equation (5.5) and $f = g = 1$ in equation (5.6), the model has 33 parameters to be estimated. If we introduce one more variable in the model (like the interest rate), then we would have to estimate 81 parameters. Moreover, the tests that we conduct in Section 5.4 indicate that the exclusion of such a variable is not expected to result in significant misspecification error.

In order to estimate our bivariate GARCH-in-Mean asymmetric BEKK model, we construct the likelihood function, ignoring the constant term and assuming that the statistical innovations are conditionally Gaussian

$$l_t = -\frac{1}{2} \sum_{t=t+1}^{T} \log |H_t| - \frac{1}{2} \sum_{t=t+1}^{T} \left(e_t' H_t^{-1} e_t \right)$$

where e_t and H_t are evaluated at their estimates. The log-likelihood is maximized with respect to the parameters Γ_i $(i = 1, \cdots, p)$, Ψ_j $(j = 1, \cdots, q)$, C, B, A, and D. As we are using the BEKK model, we do not need to impose any restrictions on the variance parameters to make H_t positive definite. Moreover, we are estimating all the parameters simultaneously rather than estimating mean and variance parameters separately, thus avoiding the Lee *et al.* (1995) problem of generated regressors.

5.4   Empirical Evidence

Initially we used the AIC and SIC criteria to select the optimal values of p and q in (5.5). However, because of computational difficulties and remaining serial correlation and ARCH effects in the standardized residuals, we set $p = 3$ and $q = 1$ in equation (5.5). Hence, with $p = 3$ and $q = 1$ in equation

(5.5), and $f = g = 1$ in equation (5.6), we estimate a total of 37 parameters. Maximum likelihood (ML) estimates of the parameters and diagnostic test statistics are presented in Tables 5.2 and 5.3.

We conduct a battery of misspecification tests, using robustified versions of the standard test statistics based on the standardized residuals,

$$z_i = \frac{e_{i,t}}{\sqrt{\hat{h}_{ij,t}}}, \qquad \text{for } i, j = \Delta \ln y, \, \Delta \ln oil.$$

As shown in panel A of Table 5.2, the Ljung-Box Q-statistics for testing serial correlation cannot reject the null hypothesis of no autocorrelation (at conventional significance levels) for the values and the squared values of the standardized residuals, suggesting that there is no evidence of conditional heteroscedasticity. Moreover, the failure of the data to reject the null hypotheses of $E(z) = 0$ and $E(z^2) = 1$, implicitly indicates that our bivariate asymmetric GARCH-in-Mean model does not bear significant misspecification error — see, for example, Kroner and Ng (1998).

In Table 5.3, we also present diagnostic tests suggested by Engle and Ng (1993) and Kroner and Ng (1998), based on the 'generalized residuals,' defined as $e_{i,t}e_{j,t} - h_{ij,t}$ for $i, j = \Delta \ln y, \, \Delta \ln oil$. For all symmetric GARCH models, the news impact curve — see Engle and Ng (1993) — is symmetric and centered at $e_{i,t-1} = 0$. A generalized residual can be thought of as the distance between a point on the scatter plot of $e_{i,t}e_{j,t}$ from a corresponding point on the news impact curve. If the conditional heteroscedasticity part of the model is correct, $E_{t-1}(e_{i,t}e_{j,t} - h_{ij,t}) = 0$ for all values of i and j, generalized residuals should be uncorrelated with all information known at time $t - 1$. In other words, the unconditional expectation of $e_{i,t}e_{j,t}$ should be equal to its conditional one, $h_{ij,t}$.

The Engle and Ng (1993) and Kroner and Ng (1998) misspecification indicators test whether we can predict the generalized residuals by some variables observed in the past, but which are not included in the model — this is exactly the intuition behind $E_{t-1}(e_{i,t}e_{j,t} - h_{ij,t}) = 0$. In this regard, we follow Kroner and Ng (1998) and Shields *et al.* (2005) and define two sets of misspecification indicators. In a two dimensional space, we first partition $(e_{\Delta \ln y, t-1}, \, e_{\Delta \ln oil, t-1})$ into four quadrants in terms of the possible sign of the two residuals. Then, to shed light on any possible sign bias of the model, we define the first set of indicator functions as $I(e_{\Delta \ln y, t-1} < 0)$, $I(e_{\Delta \ln oil, t-1} < 0)$, $I(e_{\Delta \ln y, t-1} < 0; \, e_{\Delta \ln oil, t-1} < 0)$, $I(e_{\Delta \ln y, t-1} > 0; \, e_{\Delta \ln oil, t-1} < 0)$, $I(e_{\Delta \ln y, t-1} < 0; \, e_{\Delta \ln oil, t-1} > 0)$ and $I(e_{\Delta \ln y, t-1} > 0; \, e_{\Delta \ln oil, t-1} > 0)$, where $I(\cdot)$ equals one if the ar-

gument is true and zero otherwise. Significance of any of these indicator functions indicates that the model (5.5)-(5.6) is incapable of predicting the effects of some shocks to either $\Delta \ln y_t$ or $\Delta \ln oil_t$. Moreover,
due to the fact that the possible effect of a shock could be a function
of both the size and the sign of the shock, we define a second set of in-
dicator functions, $e^2_{\Delta \ln y_{t-1}} I(e_{\Delta \ln y,t-1} < 0)$, $e^2_{\Delta \ln y,t-1} I(e_{\Delta \ln oil,t-1} < 0)$,
$e^2_{\Delta \ln oil,t-1} I(e_{\Delta \ln y,t-1} < 0)$, and $e^2_{\Delta \ln oil,t-1} I(e_{\Delta \ln oil,t-1} < 0)$. These indicators are technically scaled versions of the former ones, with the magnitude
of the shocks as a scale measure.

We conducted indicator tests and report the results in Table 5.3. As can
be seen in Table 5.3, most of the indicators fail to reject the null hypothesis
of no misspecification — all test statistics in Table 5.3 are distributed as
$\chi^2(1)$. Hence, our model (5.5)-(5.6) captures the effects of all sign bias
and sign-size scale depended shocks in predicting volatility and there is
no significant misspecification error. This means that the exclusion of the
interest rate variable (in y_t), mentioned earlier, is not expected to lead to
significant misspecification problems.

Turning now back to panel B of Table 5.2, the diagonality restriction,
$\gamma^{(i)}_{12} = \gamma^{(i)}_{21} = 0$ for $i = 1, 2, 3$, is rejected, meaning that the data provide
strong evidence of the existence of dynamic interactions between $\Delta \ln y_{t-1}$
and $\Delta \ln oil_t$. The null hypothesis of homoscedastic disturbances requires
the A, B, and D matrices to be jointly insignificant (that is, $\alpha_{ij} = \beta_{ij} =
\delta_{ij} = 0$ for all i,j) and is rejected at the 1% level or better, suggesting
that there is significant conditional heteroscedasticity in the data. The null
hypothesis of symmetric conditional variance-covariances, which requires
all elements of the D matrix to be jointly insignificant (that is, $\delta_{ij} = 0$ for
all i,j), is rejected at the 1% level or better, implying the existence of some
asymmetries in the data which the model is capable of capturing. Also, the
null hypothesis of a diagonal covariance process requires the off-diagonal
elements of the A, B, and D matrices to be jointly insignificant (that is,
$\alpha_{12} = \alpha_{21} = \beta_{12} = \beta_{21} = \delta_{12} = \delta_{21} = 0$), but these estimated coefficients
are jointly significant at the 1% level of significance.

Thus the $\Delta \ln y_t$-$\Delta \ln oil_t$ process is strongly conditionally heteroscedastic, with innovations to oil price changes significantly influencing the conditional variance of output growth in an asymmetric way. Moreover, the
sign as well as the size of oil price change innovations are important. To
establish the relationship between the volatility in the change in the price
of oil and output growth, in Table 5.2 we test the null hypothesis that the
volatility of $\Delta \ln oil_t$ does not (Granger) cause output growth, $H_0 : \psi_{12} = 0$.

We strongly reject the null hypothesis, finding strong evidence in support of the hypothesis that $\Delta \ln oil_t$ volatility Granger causes output growth.

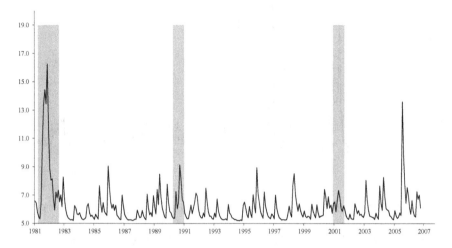

Fig. 5.3   Conditional Standard Deviation of Output Growth

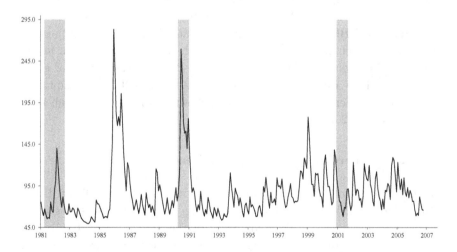

Fig. 5.4   Conditional Standard Deviation of the Change in the Price of Oil

In Figures 5.3, 5.4, and 5.5 we plot the conditional standard deviations of output growth and the change in the price of oil as well as the conditional covariance implied by our estimates of the asymmetric VAR-BEKK model in Table 5.2. In Figure 5.3, the biggest episode of output growth volatility

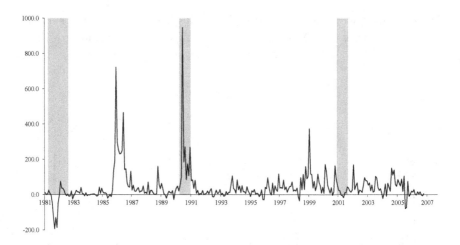

Fig. 5.5   Covariance Between Output Growth and the Change in the Price of Oil

coincides with the 2009 NBER recession — the biggest recession in the sample. Regarding the change in the real price of oil, $\Delta \ln Oil_t$, Figure 5.4 shows that the biggest episodes of oil price change volatility took place in 1986, 1990, and 2009. All of these volatility jumps in $\Delta \ln Oil_t$ do not coincide with NBER recessions, but the relatively higher volatility jump in the oil price change in 2009 coincides with the biggest recession in the sample. The volatility jumps in 1986 and 1999 are the results of steep oil price declines rather than oil price increases. Finally, the conditional covariance between $\Delta \ln y_t$ and $\Delta \ln Oil_t$, shown in Figure 5.5, is highest in 1986, 1991, and 2009.

5.5   Generalized Impulse Response Functions

As van Dijk et al. (2007) recently put it, "it generally is difficult, if not impossible, to fully understand and interpret nonlinear time series models by considering the estimated values of the model parameters only." Thus, in order to quantify the dynamic response of output growth and oil price changes to shocks and to investigate the statistical significance of the asymmetry in the variance-covariance structure, we calculate Generalized Impulse Response Functions (GIRFs), introduced by Koop et al. (1996) and recently used by Grier et al. (2004), based on our bivariate, GARCH-in-Mean, asymmetric VAR-BEKK model (5.5)-(5.6).

Traditional impulse response functions, which are more usefully applied to linear models than to nonlinear ones, measure the effect of a shock (say of size δ) hitting the system at time t on the state of the system at time $t + n$, given that no other shocks hit the system. As Koop *et al.* (1996, p. 121) put it, "the idea is very similar to Keynesian multiplier analysis, with the difference that the analysis is carried out with respect to shocks or 'innovations' of macroeconomic time series, rather than the series themselves (such as investment or government expenditure)." In the case of multivariate nonlinear models, however, traditional impulse response functions depend on the sign and size of the shock as well as the history of the system (i.e., expansionary or contractionary) before the shock hits — see, for example, Potter (2000).

In our asymmetric bivariate, GARCH-in-Mean, VAR-BEKK model, shocks impact on output growth and the change in the price of oil through the conditional mean as described in equation (5.5) and with lags through the conditional variance as described in equation (5.6). Moreover, the impulse responses of $\Delta \ln y_t$ and $\Delta \ln Oil_t$ depend on the composition of the $e_{\Delta \ln y_t}$ and $e_{\Delta \ln oil_t}$ shocks — that is, the effect of a shock to $\Delta \ln Oil_t$ is not isolated from having a contemporaneous effect on $\Delta \ln y_t$ and vice versa. The GIRFs that we use in this chapter provide a method of dealing with the problems of shock, history, and composition dependence of impulse responses in multivariate (linear and) nonlinear models.

In particular, assuming that $\boldsymbol{y}_t$ is a random vector, the GIRF for an arbitrary current shock, $\boldsymbol{v}_t$, and history, ω_{t-1}, is defined as

$$\text{GIRF}_{\boldsymbol{y}}(n, \boldsymbol{v}_t, \omega_{t-1}) = E\left[\boldsymbol{y}_{t+n} | \boldsymbol{v}_t, \omega_{t-1}\right] - E\left[\boldsymbol{y}_{t+n} | \omega_{t-1}\right] \qquad (5.7)$$

for $n = 0, 1, 2, \cdots$. Assuming that $\boldsymbol{v}_t$ and ω_{t-1} are realizations of the random variables $\boldsymbol{V}_t$ and Ω_{t-1} (where Ω_{t-1} is the set containing information used to forecast $\boldsymbol{y}_t$) that generate realizations of $\{\boldsymbol{y}_t\}$, then according to Koop *et al.* (1996), the GIRF in (5.7) can be considered to be a realization of a random variable defined by

$$\text{GIRF}_{\boldsymbol{y}}(n, \boldsymbol{V}_t, \Omega_{t-1}) = E\left[\boldsymbol{y}_{t+n} | \boldsymbol{V}_t, \Omega_{t-1}\right] - E\left[\boldsymbol{y}_{t+n} | \Omega_{t-1}\right]. \qquad (5.8)$$

Equation (5.8) is the difference between two conditional expectations. It is also to be noted that generalized impulse responses are expected values (which are not random values and will not have error bands).

The computation of GIRFs in the case of multivariate nonlinear models is made difficult by the inability to construct analytical expressions for the conditional expectations, $E\left[\boldsymbol{y}_{t+n} | \boldsymbol{V}_t, \Omega_{t-1}\right]$ and $E\left[\boldsymbol{y}_{t+n} | \Omega_{t-1}\right]$, in equation (5.8). To deal with this problem, Monte Carlo methods of stochastic

Oil Price Uncertainty

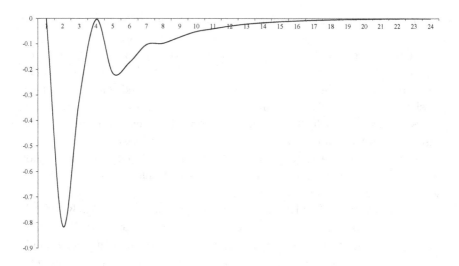

Fig. 5.6   GIRF of Output Growth to an Oil Price Change Shock

simulation are used to construct the GIRFs. Here, we allow for time-varying composition dependence and follow the algorithm described in Koop *et al.* (1996). In particular, using 310 data points as histories, we first transform the estimated residuals by using the variance-covariance structure and Jordan decomposition. Then at each history, 50 realizations are drawn randomly, thereby obtaining identical and independent distributions over time. Recovering the time varying dependence among the residuals, 15500 realizations of impulse responses are calculated for each horizon. Finally, the whole process is replicated 150 times to average out the effects of impulses.

The GIRFs to an average shock in $\Delta \ln y_t$ and $\Delta \ln oil_t$ are shown in Figures 5.6 and 5.7 — they show the effect on $\Delta \ln y_t$ and $\Delta \ln oil_t$ of an average initial shock in $\Delta \ln y_t$ and $\Delta \ln oil_t$. As can be seen, none of the shocks is very persistent, although the shock to $\Delta \ln oil_t$ on $\Delta \ln y_t$ is more persistent than the shock to $\Delta \ln y_t$ on $\Delta \ln oil_t$, as it takes longer for $\Delta \ln y_t$ to return to its original value. Shocks to output growth and the change in the price of oil provide a large stimulus to $\Delta \ln y_t$ and $\Delta \ln oil_t$ for the first few months. In particular, in response to an oil price change shock, output growth declines by more than 0.75% in the first quarter of the year and returns to its mean within one and a half years. Also the change in the price of oil responds very strongly (almost around 12%) to the innovation in output growth within the first few months of the year.

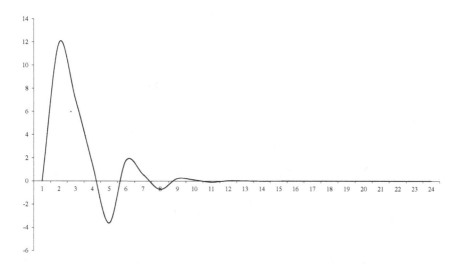

Fig. 5.7 GIRF of the Oil Price Change to an Output Growth Shock

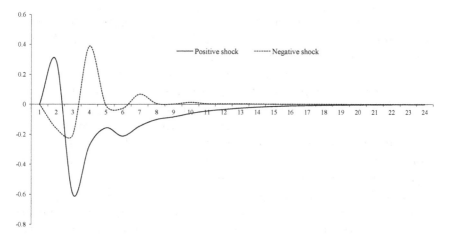

Fig. 5.8 GIRFs of Output Growth to Positive and Negative Shocks to the Change in the Price of Oil

In Figures 5.8 and 5.9, we differentiate between positive and negative shocks, in order to address issues regarding the asymmetry of shocks. As can be seen in Figure 5.8, output growth declines due to a positive $\Delta \ln oil_t$ shock and increases in response to a negative $\Delta \ln oil_t$ shock. The responses are not the mirror image of each other, suggesting that output growth,

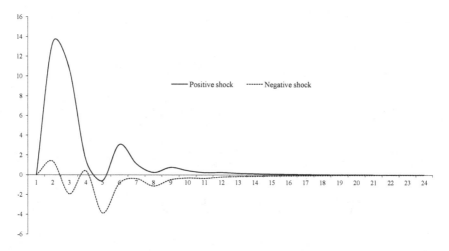

Fig. 5.9   GIRFs of the Change in the Price of Oil to Positive and Negative Output Growth Shocks

$\Delta \ln y_t$, responds asymmetrically to shocks in the change in the price of oil, $\Delta \ln oil_t$. Also the response of output growth to a negative $\Delta \ln oil_t$ shock returns to zero faster than to a positive shock of equal magnitude, suggesting that positive shocks in the change in the price of oil have more persistent effects on output growth than negative ones. Figure 5.9 shows the GIRFs of $\Delta \ln oil_t$ to positive and negative output growth shocks. A positive $\Delta \ln y_t$ shock raises $\Delta \ln oil_t$ and a negative $\Delta \ln y_t$ shock lowers $\Delta \ln oil_t$. The response of $\Delta \ln oil_t$ to output growth shocks is also asymmetric — a positive output growth shock has a larger effect on the change in the price of oil compared to a negative $\Delta \ln y_t$ shock.

Given the asymmetric nature of the specification of our bivariate asymmetric VAR-BEKK model, we follow van Dijk *et al.* (2007) and use the GIRFs to positive and negative shocks to compute a random asymmetry measure, defined as follows,

$$\mathrm{ASY}_{\boldsymbol{y}}(n, \boldsymbol{V}_t^+, \Omega_{t-1}) = \mathrm{GIRF}_{\boldsymbol{y}}(n, \boldsymbol{V}_t^+, \Omega_{t-1})$$
$$+ \mathrm{GIRF}_{\boldsymbol{y}}(n, -\boldsymbol{V}_t^+, \Omega_{t-1}) \qquad (5.9)$$

where $\mathrm{GIRF}_{\boldsymbol{y}}(n, \boldsymbol{V}_t^+, \Omega_{t-1})$ denotes the GIRF derived from conditioning on the set of all possible positive shocks, $\mathrm{GIRF}_{\boldsymbol{y}}(n, -\boldsymbol{V}_t^+, \Omega_{t-1})$ denotes the GIRF derived from conditioning on the set of all possible negative shocks, and $\boldsymbol{V}_t^+ = \{\boldsymbol{v}_t | \boldsymbol{v}_t > 0\}$. The distribution of $\mathrm{ASY}(n, \boldsymbol{V}_t^+, \Omega_{t-1})$ can provide

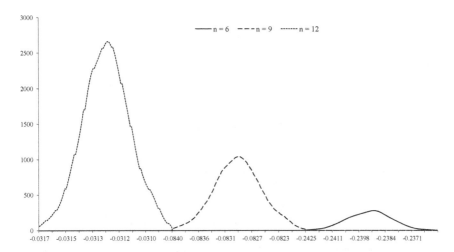

Fig. 5.10   The Distribution of the Asymmetry Measure Based on the GIRFs of Output Growth to Shocks in the Change in the Price of Oil

an indication of the asymmetric effects of positive and negative shocks. In particular, if $\mathrm{ASY}(n, V_t^+, \Omega_{t-1})$ has a symmetric distribution with a mean of zero, then positive and negative shocks have exactly the same effect (with opposite sign).

We have computed the asymmetry measures for $\Delta \ln y_t$ and $\Delta \ln oil_t$ and show the distributions of the respective $\mathrm{ASY}_y(n, V_t^+, \Omega_{t-1})$ measures in Figures 5.10 and 5.11 at horizons $n = 6$, $n = 9$, and $n = 12$. As can be seen in Figure 5.10, on average output growth exhibits more persistence to a positive $\Delta \ln oil_t$ shock than to a negative one. In particular, the loss of output growth due to a positive $\Delta \ln oil_t$ shock (bad news) at horizon $n = 9$ is 0.083% in excess of the gain in output growth from a negative $\Delta \ln oil_t$ shock (good news) of equal magnitude. Figure 5.11 shows the asymmetry measure for an output growth shock on $\Delta \ln oil_t$. We find a stronger effect of a positive output growth shock on the change in the price of oil than of a negative shock of equal magnitude. On average at horizon 9, the increase in $\Delta \ln oil_t$ due to a positive output growth shock is 0.256% in excess of the decrease in $\Delta \ln oil_t$ due to a negative $\Delta \ln y_t$ shock.

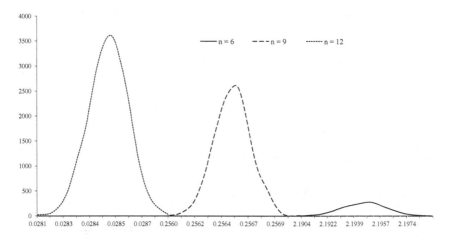

Fig. 5.11   The Distribution of the Asymmetry Measure Based on the GIRFs of the Change in the Price of Oil to Shocks in Output Growth

5.6   Volatility Impulse Response Functions

The GIRFs, introduced by Koop *et al.* (1996), trace the effects of independent shocks (or news) on the conditional mean. Recently, Hafner and Herwartz (2006) have introduced a new concept of impulse response functions, known as 'volatility impulse response functions' (VIRFs), tracing the effects of independent shocks on the conditional variance — see also Shields *et al.* (2005) for an early application of the Hafner and Herwartz (2006) VIRFs concept.

We start with the conditional variance-covariance matrix of e_t, H_t, and define $Q_t = \text{vech}(H_t)$ to be a 3×1 random vector with the following elements (in that order): $h_{\Delta \ln y, t}$, $h_{\Delta \ln y \Delta \ln oil, t}$, $h_{\Delta \ln oil, t}$. Then the VIRFs of Q_t, for $n = 0, 1, \cdots$, are given by

$$\text{VIRF}_{\boldsymbol{Q}}(n, \boldsymbol{v}_t, \omega_{t-1}) = E\left[\boldsymbol{Q}_{t+n} | \boldsymbol{v}_t, \omega_{t-1}\right] - E\left[\boldsymbol{Q}_{t+n} | \omega_{t-1}\right]. \quad (5.10)$$

Hence, the VIRF is conditional on the initial shock and history, $\boldsymbol{v}_t$ and ω_{t-1}, and constructs the response by averaging out future innovations given the past and present. Following Koop *et al.* (1996) and assuming that $\boldsymbol{v}_t$ and ω_{t-1} are realizations of the random variables $\boldsymbol{V}_t$ and Ω_{t-1} that generate realizations of $\{\boldsymbol{Q}\}$, the VIRF in (5.10) can be considered to be a realization of a random variable given by

$$\text{VIRF}_{\boldsymbol{Q}}(n, \boldsymbol{V}_t, \Omega_{t-1}) = E\left[\boldsymbol{Q}_{t+n} | \boldsymbol{V}_t, \Omega_{t-1}\right] - E\left[\boldsymbol{Q}_{t+n} | \Omega_{t-1}\right].$$

As already noted, the first element of $\text{VIRF}_Q(n, \boldsymbol{V}_t, \Omega_{t-1})$ gives the impulse response of the conditional variance of $\Delta \ln y_t$, $h_{\Delta \ln y,t}$, the second that of the conditional covariance, $h_{\Delta \ln y \Delta \ln oil,t}$, and the third that of the conditional variance of $\Delta \ln oil_t$, $h_{\Delta \ln oil,t}$. It should also be noted that in contrast to the GIRFs where positive and negative shocks produce opposite effects, VIRFs consist of the same (positive sign) effect irrespective of the sign of the shocks. Also, shock linearity does not hold in the case of VIRFs. Finally, unlike traditional impulse responses that do not depend on history, VIRFs depend on history through the conditional variance-covariance matrix at time $t = 0$ when the innovation occurs.

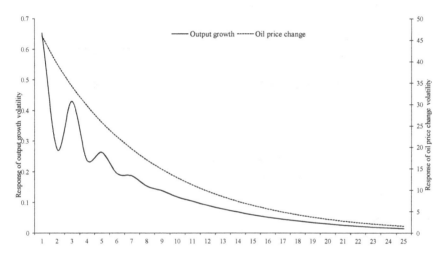

Fig. 5.12   Volatility Responses to Oil Price Change Shocks

Using an analytic version of the VIRF, as described in Hafner and Herwartz (2006), we show t he VIRFs to shocks in $\Delta \ln y_t$ and $\Delta \ln oil_t$ in Figures 5.12 and 5.13. In Figure 5.12 (the responses of oil price change volatility are on the secondary y-axis), shocks to the change in the price of oil, $\Delta \ln oil_t$, produce much higher responses in the conditional variance of the change in the price of oil, $h_{\Delta \ln oil,t}$, than in the conditional variance of output growth, $h_{\Delta \ln y,t}$. Moreover, the responses of both oil price change and output growth volatility are persistent — they take more than two years to return to zero. In Figure 5.13 (again the responses of oil price change volatility are on the secondary y-axis), shocks to output growth have also a very remarkable impact on the conditional variance of the change in the price of oil, $h_{\Delta \ln oil,t}$, and the conditional variance of output growth,

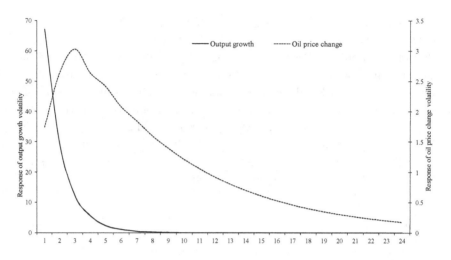

Fig. 5.13   Volatility Responses to Output Growth Shocks

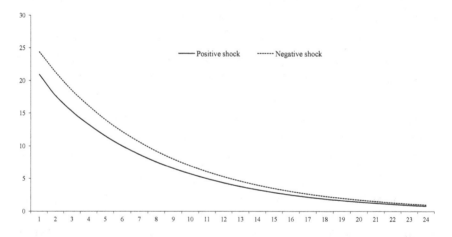

Fig. 5.14   VIRFs of Oil Price Change to Positive and Negative Shocks to the Change in the Price of Oil

$h_{\Delta \ln y,t}$. The peak response of the change in the price of oil is much lower than that of output growth volatility and $h_{\Delta \ln oil,t}$ takes longer to return to its original position compared to $h_{\Delta \ln y,t}$. In Figure 5.14, we differentiate again between positive and negative shocks in order to investigate the asymmetry of shocks on the conditional variance of the change in the real price of oil. As it is shown, negative oil price shocks have a larger impact

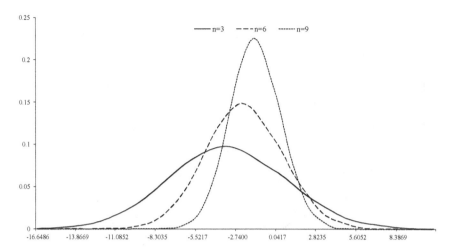

Fig. 5.15 The Distribution of the Asymmetry Measure Based on the VIRFs of the Change in Price of Oil to Shocks in the Change in the Price of Oil

on oil price change volatility than positive oil price shocks do.

As with the GIRFs, we use the VIRFs to positive and negative innovations to compute the following random asymmetry measure

$$\text{ASY}_{\boldsymbol{Q}}(n, \boldsymbol{V}_t^+, \Omega_{t-1}) = \text{VIRF}_{\boldsymbol{Q}}(n, \boldsymbol{V}_t^+, \Omega_{t-1})$$
$$- \text{VIRF}_{\boldsymbol{Q}}(n, -\boldsymbol{V}_t^+, \Omega_{t-1}) \qquad (5.11)$$

where $\text{VIRF}_{\boldsymbol{Q}}(n, \boldsymbol{V}_t^+, \Omega_{t-1})$ denotes the VIRF derived from conditioning on the set of all possible positive innovations, $\text{VIRF}_{\boldsymbol{Q}}(n, -\boldsymbol{V}_t^+, \Omega_{t-1})$ denotes the VIRF derived from conditioning on the set of all possible negative innovations, and $\boldsymbol{V}_t^+ = \{\boldsymbol{v}_t | \boldsymbol{v}_t > 0\}$. The distribution of $\text{ASY}_{\boldsymbol{Q}}(n, \boldsymbol{V}_t^+, \Omega_{t-1})$ will be centered at zero if positive and negative shocks have exactly the same effect. The difference between the random asymmetry measures (5.9) and (5.11) is that the latter is the difference between $\text{VIRF}_{\boldsymbol{Q}}(n, \boldsymbol{V}_t^+, \Omega_{t-1})$ and $\text{VIRF}_{\boldsymbol{Q}}(n, -\boldsymbol{V}_t^+, \Omega_{t-1})$ whereas the former is the sum of $\text{GIRF}_{\boldsymbol{y}}(n, \boldsymbol{V}_t^+, \Omega_{t-1})$ and $\text{GIRF}_{\boldsymbol{y}}(n, -\boldsymbol{V}_t^+, \Omega_{t-1})$. This is so because unlike the GIRFs where positive and negative shocks cause the response functions to take opposite signs, the VIRFs are made up of the squares of the innovations and are thus of the same sign.

We have computed the asymmetry measures $\text{ASY}_{\boldsymbol{Q}}(n, \boldsymbol{V}_t^+, \Omega_{t-1})$ and show the distributions of these measures in Figures 5.15 and 5.16, at horizon $n = 3, 6, 9$. The distribution in Figure 5.15 indicates that on average negative shocks to the change in the price of oil have more persistent effects

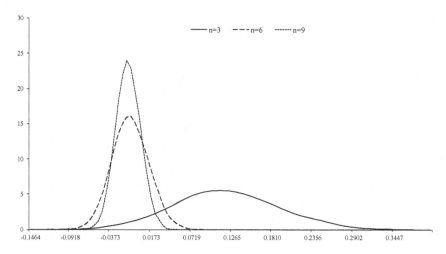

Fig. 5.16   The Distribution of the Asymmetry Measure Based on the VIRFs of the Change in the Price of Oil to Shocks in Output Growth

on oil price change volatility than positive shocks do. The asymmetry measure for an oil price change shock to oil price change volatility at horizon $n = 3$ is -4.13%. Given the negative relationship between oil price change volatility and output growth, this asymmetric response of oil price change volatility tends to further weaken the short run response of output growth to lower oil prices. This result further helps in explaining the asymmetric response of output growth to oil price shocks. Also, in Figure 5.16, positive shocks to the change in the price of oil have more persistent effects on the volatility of output growth than negative shocks do. The asymmetry measure for oil price change shocks to the volatility in the change in the price of oil at horizon $n = 3$ is 0.13%.

5.7   Conclusion

Recent empirical research regarding the relationship between the price of oil and real economic activity has focused on the role of uncertainty about oil prices — see, for example, Elder and Serletis (2010). In this chapter, we examine the effects of oil price uncertainty and its asymmetry on real economic activity in the United States, in the context of a vector autoregression, in output growth and the change in the real price of oil, because the identification of higher order VARs is usually highly questionable. In doing so, we modify our bivariate VAR to accommodate asymmetric GARCH-in-Mean errors.

Our model is extremely general and allows for the possibilities of spillovers and asymmetries in the variance-covariance structure for real output growth and the change in the real price of oil. Our measure of oil price uncertainty is the conditional variance of the oil price change forecast error. We isolate the effects of volatility in the change in the price of oil and its asymmetry on output growth and, following Koop *et al.* (1996), Hafner and Herwartz (2006), and van Dijk *et al.* (2007) we employ simulation methods to calculate Generalized Impulse Response Functions (GIRFs) and Volatility Impulse Response Functions (VIRFs) to trace the effects of independent shocks on the conditional mean and the conditional variance, respectively, of output growth and the change in the real price of oil.

We find that our bivariate, GARCH-in-Mean, asymmetric BEKK model embodies a reasonable description of the United States data on output growth and the change in the real price of oil. We show that the conditional variance-covariance process underlying output growth and the change in the real price of oil exhibits significant non-diagonality and asymmetry. We present evidence that increased uncertainty about the change in the real price of oil is associated with a lower average growth rate of real economic activity. Generalized impulse response experiments highlight the asymmetric effects of positive and negative shocks in the change in the real price of oil to output growth. Also, volatility impulse response experiments reveal that the effect of good news (negative shocks to the change in the real price of oil) on the conditional variance of the change in the real price of oil differs in magnitude and persistence from that of bad news of similar magnitude. This helps further in explaining the asymmetric response of output growth to oil price change shocks.

Oil Price Uncertainty

Table 5.1 Summary Statistics

A. Summary Statistics

Variable	Mean	Variance	Skewness	Excess kurtosis	J-B normality
$\Delta \ln y_t$	1.951	70.174	-0.956	4.375	348.789
					(0.000)
$\Delta \ln oil_t$	-0.607	9583.058	-0.344	3.374	181.375
					(0.000)

B. Unit Root and Stationary Tests

Variable	Unit root tests			KPSS stationarity tests	
	$\mathrm{ADF}(\tau)$	$\mathrm{ADF}(\mu)$	ADF	$\widehat{\eta}_\mu$	$\widehat{\eta}_\tau$
$\Delta \ln y_t$	-6.508	-6.898	-6.898	0.181	0.155
$\Delta \ln oil_t$	-8.274	-8.265	-8.459	0.200	0.019
5% cv	-1.941	-2.871	-3.425	0.463	0.146

C. Tests for Serial Correlation and ARCH

Variable	Q(4)	Q(12)	ARCH(4)
$\Delta \ln y_t$	100.734	127.531	28.192
	(0.000)	(0.000)	(0.000)
$\Delta \ln oil_t$	33.913	50.807	27.187
	(0.000)	(0.000)	(0.000)

D. Engle and Ng (1993) Tests for Sign and Size Bias in Variance

Variable	Sign	Negative size	Positive size	Joint
$\Delta \ln y_t$	24.440	-7.846	-1.622	37.102
	(0.013)	(0.000)	(0.171)	(0.000)
$\Delta \ln oil_t$	3543.713	-87.300	-0.786	32.087
	(0.062)	(0.000)	(0.963)	(0.000)

Note: Numbers in parentheses are tail areas of tests. Annualized logarithmic first differences are used.

Table 5.2 The Bivariate Garch-In-Mean Asymmetric BEKK Model

Model: Equations (5.5) and (5.6) with $p = 3$, $q = 1$, and $f = g = 1$

A. Conditional mean equation

$$
\mathbf{a} = \begin{bmatrix} 0.725 \\ (0.895) \\ -47.680 \\ (0.005) \end{bmatrix} ; \boldsymbol{\Gamma}_1 = \begin{bmatrix} 0.213 & 0.002 \\ (0.000) & (0.614) \\ 0.528 & 0.174 \\ (0.303) & (0.000) \end{bmatrix} ;
$$

$$
\boldsymbol{\Gamma}_2 = \begin{bmatrix} 0.263 & -0.006 \\ (0.000) & (0.027) \\ 1.633 & -0.100 \\ (0.000) & (0.112) \end{bmatrix} ; \boldsymbol{\Gamma}_3 = \begin{bmatrix} 0.179 & -0.002 \\ (0.163) & (0.824) \\ -0.276 & 0.043 \\ (0.512) & (0.380) \end{bmatrix} ;
$$

Residual diagnostics

	Mean	Variance	$Q(4)$	$Q^2(4)$	$Q(12)$	$Q^2(12)$
z_{y_t}	−0.007	0.994	1.139	2.701	15.358	12.029
	(0.892)	(0.997)	(0.887)	(0.608)	(0.222)	(0.443)
z_{oil_t}	−0.020	1.003	7.016	2.650	13.517	8.868
	(0.698)	(1.001)	(0.135)	(0.617)	(0.332)	(0.714)

Note: Numbers in parentheses are tail areas of tests.

Table 5.2 cont'd

Model: Equations (5.5) and (5.6) with $p = 3$, $q = 1$, and $f = g = 1$

B. Conditional variance-covariance structure

$$C = \begin{bmatrix} 5.400 & -3.338 \\ (0.000) & (0.435) \\ & 22.662 \\ & (0.001) \end{bmatrix} \; ; B = \begin{bmatrix} 0.002 & 1.213 \\ (0.994) & (0.354) \\ 0.001 & 0.807 \\ (0.919) & (0.000) \end{bmatrix} \; ;$$

$$A = \begin{bmatrix} 0.393 & 0.298 \\ (0.277) & (0.842) \\ 0.018 & 0.546 \\ (0.133) & (0.000) \end{bmatrix} \; ; D = \begin{bmatrix} -0.898 & 1.491 \\ (0.000) & (0.093) \\ -0.016 & 0.037 \\ (0.335) & (0.752) \end{bmatrix} .$$

Hypothesis testing

Diagonal VAR	$H_0 : \gamma_{12}^{(i)} = \gamma_{21}^{(i)} = 0$, for $i = 1, 2, 3$	(0.000)
No GARCH	$H_0 : \alpha_{ij} = \beta_{ij} = \delta_{ij} = 0$, for all i, j	(0.000)
No GARCH-M	$H_0 : \psi_{ij}^{k} = 0$, for all i, j, k	(0.000)
No asymmetry	$H_0 : \delta_{ij} = 0$, for $i, j = 1, 2$	(0.000)
Diagonal GARCH	$H_0 : \alpha_{12} = \alpha_{21} = \beta_{12} = \beta_{21} = \delta_{12} = \delta_{21} = 0$	(0.000)

Note: Numbers in parentheses are tail areas of tests.

Table 5.3 Diagnostic Tests Based on the News Impact Curve

	$e^2_{\Delta \ln y, t}$ $-h_{\Delta \ln y \Delta \ln y, t}$	$e_{\Delta \ln y, t} e_{\Delta \ln oil, t}$ $-h_{\Delta \ln y \Delta \ln oil, t}$	$e^2_{\Delta \ln oil, t}$ $-h_{\Delta \ln oil \Delta \ln oil, t}$
$I(e_{\Delta \ln y, t-1} < 0)$	1.107 (0.292)	0.337 (0.561)	2.441 (0.118)
$I(e_{\Delta \ln oil, t-1} < 0)$	0.027 (0.867)	0.620 (0.430)	1.639 (0.200)
$I(e_{\Delta \ln y, t-1} < 0, e_{\Delta \ln oil, t-1} < 0)$	31.178 (0.000)	5.890 (0.015)	0.772 (0.379)
$I(e_{\Delta \ln y, t-1} > 0, e_{\Delta \ln oil, t-1} < 0)$	18.607 (0.000)	12.271 (0.000)	3.187 (0.074)
$I(e_{\Delta \ln y, t-1} < 0, e_{\Delta \ln oil, t-1} > 0)$	1.414 (0.234)	20.550 (0.000)	8.859 (0.003)
$I(e_{\Delta \ln y, t-1} > 0, e_{\Delta \ln oil, t-1} > 0)$	1.322 (0.250)	3.452 (0.063)	1.205 (0.272)
$e^2_{\Delta \ln y, t-1} I(e_{\Delta \ln y, t-1} < 0)$	0.392 (0.530)	1.954 (0.162)	2.953 (0.085)
$e^2_{\Delta \ln y, t-1} I(e_{\Delta \ln oil, t-1} < 0)$	0.688 (0.407)	5.476 (0.019)	10.516 (0.001)
$e^2_{\Delta \ln oil, t-1} I(e_{\Delta \ln y, t-1} < 0)$	0.350 (0.553)	0.514 (0.473)	0.009 (0.923)
$e^2_{\Delta \ln oil, t-1} I(e_{\Delta \ln oil, t-1} < 0)$	0.153 (0.695)	2.536 (0.111)	1.826 (0.176)

Note: Numbers in parentheses are tail areas of tests.

Chapter 6

Evidence from Canada*

6.1   Introduction

In Chapter 4 we examined the direct effects of oil price uncertainty on real economic activity in the United States in the context of a structural vector autoregression (VAR) that is modified to accommodate GARCH-in-Mean errors, as detailed in Engle and Kroner (1995) and Elder (2004). Also, in Chapter 5 we investigated the asymmetric effects of uncertainty on output growth and oil price changes as well as the response of uncertainty about output growth and oil price changes to positive and negative oil price shocks. Both Chapters 4 and 5 use U.S. data and a bivariate VAR modified to accommodate GARCH-in-Mean errors, as detailed in Engle and Kroner (1995), Grier, Henry, Olekalns, and Shields (2004), and Shields, Olekalns, Henry, and Brooks (2005). They present evidence that increased uncertainty about the change in the price of oil is associated with a lower average growth rate of real economic activity. The evidence is consistent with earlier theoretical and empirical findings — see, for example, Bernanke (1983), Lee, Ni, and Ratti (1995), Ferderer (1996), and Edelstein and Killian (2007). More recently, however, Kilian and Vigfusson (2011a,b) investigate whether the impulse responses of U.S. real GDP over the post-1973 period are asymmetric to oil price increases and decreases and find no evidence against the null hypothesis of symmetric response functions.

In this chapter we build on the previous two chapters and investigate the relationship between the price of oil and the level of economic activity in Canada, using quarterly data over the period from 1974:1 to 2010:1 that includes the increased volatility in oil prices in the aftermath of the financial crisis and the global recession. In doing so, we use a bivariate VARMA, GARCH-in-Mean, asymmetric BEKK model, as detailed in Engle and Kroner (1995), Grier *et al.* (2004), and Shields *et al.* (2005). We show that the conditional variance-covariance process underlying output growth and the change in the real price of oil exhibits significant non-diagonality and asymmetry, and present evidence that oil price volatility amplifies the negative effects of positive oil price shocks and attenuates the positive effects of negative oil price shocks on the level of economic activity.

This chapter differs from Chapters 4 and 5. In particular, it investigates the effects of oil price uncertainty on output in a small, oil exporting economy. It uses a (more general) bivariate VARMA, GARCH-in-Mean, asymmetric BEKK model whereas in Chapter 5 we used U.S. data and a bivariate VAR, GARCH-in-Mean, asymmetric BEKK model. The VARMA framework used in this chapter allows us to capture features of the data generating process in a more parsimonious way without adding a large number of parameters (or lagged variables) as, for example, in Cushman and Zha (1997). This chapter is also different from Chapter 4, as that chapter considers only the effects of oil price uncertainty in the mean equation for output, omitting the uncertainty of the other variable by allowing zero restrictions. Moreover, in this chapter we allow for the possibility of spillovers and asymmetries in the variance-covariance structure for real activity and the real price of oil. Finally, this chapter uses an updated sample that includes the increased volatility in oil prices since 2008, the recent recession (from October, 2008 to June, 2009), and also investigates the robustness of the results to alternative measures of the level of economic activity, alternative measures of the price of oil, and alternative data frequencies.

The chapter is organized as follows. Section 6.2 presents the data and Section 6.3 provides a brief description of the bivariate VARMA, GARCH-in-Mean, asymmetric BEKK model. Section 6.4 assesses the appropriateness of the econometric methodology by various information criteria and presents and discusses the empirical results. The final section concludes.

6.2   The Data

We use quarterly data for Canada, from the International Financial Statistics (IFS) database, maintained by the International Monetary Fund (IMF) on two variables: real GDP and the real price of oil. As demonstrated in Kilian and Vigfusson (2011a) and Alquist, Kilian, and Vigfusson (2011), during the pre-1973 period the nominal price of crude oil had only been adjusted at discrete intervals, meaning the oil price series was a discontinuous process. Although this problem is mitigated by deflating the nominal price of oil and adjusting for the exchange rate, this would imply that fluctuations in the price of oil derive entirely from price level and exchange rate movements (although the Canadian dollar was also fixed between 1962 and 1970) in the time interval over which the oil price was flat. Hence, oil price uncertainty during this part of the sample would not really derive from the oil price but rather from exchange rate and (to a larger extent) inflation uncertainty which is why we discard the pre-1973 data and use data over the period from 1974:1 to 2010:1.

In particular, we use the spot price on West Texas Intermediate (WTI) crude oil, converted to Canadian dollars, as the nominal price of oil and divide it by the consumer price index (CPI) to obtain the real price of oil.

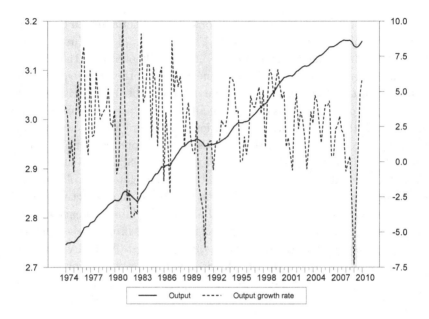

Fig. 6.1   Logged Real Output and its Rate of Growth

Regarding our choice of the WTI crude oil price, as Kilian and Vigfusson (2011a, p. 342) put it, "leading candidates for the oil price series include the price of West Texas Intermediate crude oil, the U.S. producer price of crude oil, and the U.S. refiners' acquisition cost available for imported crude oil, for domestic crude oil, and for a composite of domestic and imported crude oil. There is no general consensus on which price of oil to use." Moreover, in Chapter 4, in investigating the effects of oil price uncertainty on real economic activity we report robustness of results to alternative measures of the price of oil.

Panel A of Table 6.1 presents summary statistics for the annualized logarithmic first differences of real output and the real price of oil, denoted as y_t and o_t, and Figures 6.1 and 6.2 plot the logged levels and the logarithmic first differences of real output and the real price of oil, respectively, with shaded area indicating recessions. Statistics Canada, a federal agency, has been dating Canadian recessions since 1981. In dating these recessions, they consider the movement of all relevant economic variables that affect the business cycle, such as output, employment, sales and income, by simply not following the rule of thumb that a recession merely represents two successive quarters of falling real GDP. As can be seen in panel A of Table

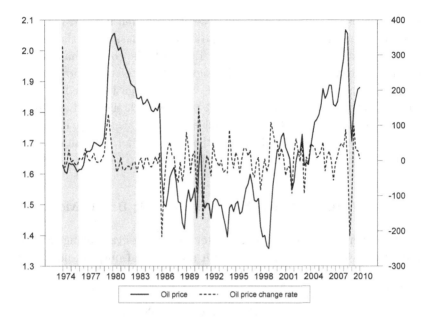

Fig. 6.2 Logged Real Oil Price and its Rate of Growth

6.1, there is significant amount of excess kurtosis present in the o_t series. Moreover, a Jarque-Bera (1980) test for normality, distributed as a $\chi^2(2)$ under the null hypothesis of normality, suggests that o_t fails to satisfy the null hypothesis of the test.

A battery of unit root and stationarity tests are conducted in panel B of Table 6.1 in the annualized logarithmic first differences of real output and the real price of oil, y_t and o_t. In particular, we report the augmented Dickey-Fuller (ADF) test [see Dickey and Fuller (1981)] and the Elliot, Rothemberg, and Stock (1996) Dickey-Fuller test with GLS detrending (DF-GLS) as well as their Point Optimal Test. Moreover, given that unit root tests have low power against relevant trend stationary alternatives, we also present Kwiatkowski *et al.* (1992) tests, known as KPSS tests, for level and trend stationarity. As can be seen, the null hypothesis of a unit root can (in general) be rejected at conventional significance levels. Moreover, the t-statistics $\widehat{\eta}_\mu$ and $\widehat{\eta}_\tau$ that test the null hypotheses of level and trend stationarity are (in general) small relative to their 5% critical values of 0.463 and 0.146 (respectively), given in Kwiatkowski *et al.* (1992). We thus conclude that y_t and o_t are stationary.

Finally, as we are interested in the asymmetry of the volatility response to news, in panel C of Table 6.1 we present Engle and Ng (1993) tests for 'sign bias,' 'negative size bias,' and 'positive size bias,' as in the previous chapter. As can be seen in panel C of Table 6.1, the conditional volatility of output growth is sensitive to the sign and size of the innovation. In particular, there is strong evidence of sign and negative size bias in the output growth volatility, and the joint test for both sign and size bias is highly significant. Also, the conditional volatility of the change in the price of oil displays negative size bias and the joint test for both sign and size bias is significant at conventional significance levels.

6.3   The VARMA, GARCH-M, Asymmetric BEKK Model

We use a version of a VARMA (vector autoregressive moving average), GARCH-in-Mean model in the growth rates of real output and the real price of oil, y_t and o_t, respectively, as follows

$$z_t = \mathbf{a} + \sum_{i=1}^{p} \Gamma_i z_{t-i} + \Psi \sqrt{h_t} + \sum_{l=1}^{q} \Theta_l e_{t-l} + e_t \qquad (6.1)$$

$$e_t | \Omega_{t-1} \sim (\mathbf{0}, \, H_t), \qquad H_t = \begin{bmatrix} h_{yy,t} & h_{yo,t} \\ h_{oy,t} & h_{oo,t} \end{bmatrix},$$

where Ω_{t-1} denotes the available information set in period $t-1$, $\mathbf{0}$ is the null vector, and

$$z_t = \begin{bmatrix} y_t \\ o_t \end{bmatrix} ; \; e_t = \begin{bmatrix} e_{y,t} \\ e_{o,t} \end{bmatrix} ; \; h_t = \begin{bmatrix} h_{yy,t} \\ h_{oo,t} \end{bmatrix} ;$$

$$\Gamma_i = \begin{bmatrix} \gamma_{11}^{(i)} & \gamma_{12}^{(i)} \\ \gamma_{21}^{(i)} & \gamma_{22}^{(i)} \end{bmatrix} ; \; \Psi = \begin{bmatrix} \psi_{11} & \psi_{12} \\ \psi_{21} & \psi_{22} \end{bmatrix} ; \; \Theta_l = \begin{bmatrix} \theta_{11}^{(l)} & \theta_{12}^{(l)} \\ \theta_{21}^{(l)} & \theta_{22}^{(l)} \end{bmatrix} .$$

Notice that we have not added any error correction term in the model as we do not find evidence of cointegration between the logged levels of output and the real price of oil, using the Engle and Granger (1987) testing approach.

Multivariate GARCH models require that we specify volatilities of y_t and o_t, measured by conditional variances. Although several different specifications have been proposed in the literature, here we follow Chapter 5 and use an asymmetric version of the BEKK model, introduced by Grier *et al.* (2004), as follows

$$H_t = C'C + \sum_{j=1}^{f} B_j' H_{t-j} B_j$$

$$+ \sum_{k=1}^{g} A_k' e_{t-k} e_{t-k}' A_k + D' u_{t-1} u_{t-1}' D, \qquad (6.2)$$

where C, B_j, A_k, and D are $n \times n$ matrices (for all values of j and k), with C being a triangular matrix to ensure positive definiteness of H. This specification allows past volatilities, H_{t-j}, as well as lagged values of ee' and uu', to show up in estimating current volatilities of output and oil, where $u_t = (u_{y,t}, u_{o,t})'$ captures potential asymmetric responses. In particular, if the price of oil is higher than expected, we take that in general to be good news for Canada, although oil price shocks may have differential effects on regional economic activity. In this regard, it should be noted that the oil and gas industry is currently the largest single private investor in Canada; in 2008 it invested \$54 billion and paid \$26 billion in taxes and royalties to governments. Moreover, it supports 500,000 jobs across the country and comprises about 25% of the Toronto Stock Exchange. We therefore capture good news about the price of oil by a positive oil price residual, by defining $u_{o,t} = \max\{e_{o,t}, 0\}$. We also capture bad news about output by defining $u_{y,t} = \min\{e_{y,t}, 0\}$.

There are $n + n^2 (p + q + 1) + n(n + 1)/2 + n^2 (f + g + 1)$ parameters in (6.1)-(6.2) and in order to deal with estimation problems in the large parameter space we assume that $f = g = 1$ in equation (6.2), consistent with recent empirical evidence regarding the superiority of GARCH(1,1) models — see, for example, Hansen and Lunde (2005).

6.4 Empirical Evidence

We estimate equations (6.1) and (6.2) using quasi maximum likelihood methods and allow necessary adjustments for standard errors by using robustified versions. We used a range of starting values to ensure that the estimation procedure converged to the global maximum. We select the optimal values of p and q in equation (6.1) in such a way that there is no serial correlation and ARCH effects in the standardized residuals of the model. In doing so, we choose $p = q = 2$ in equation (6.1) and $f = g = 1$ in equation (6.2). The inclusion of h_t in equation (6.1) allows us to investigate the effect of oil price volatility on output growth as well as the effect of output uncertainty on oil prices.

In Table 6.2 we report maximum likelihood estimates of the parameters (with p-values in parentheses) and diagnostic test statistics, based on the standardized residuals,

$$\widehat{z}_{jt} = \frac{e_{jt}}{\sqrt{\widehat{h}_{jt}}}, \qquad \text{for } j = y, o.$$

As shown in Table 6.2, the Ljung-Box (1979) Q-statistic for testing serial correlation cannot reject the null of no autocorrelation (at conventional significance levels) for the values and the squared values of the standardized residuals, suggesting that there is no significant evidence of conditional heteroscedasticity. In addition, the failure of the data to reject the null hypotheses of $E(z) = 0$ and $E(z^2) = 1$, implicitly indicates that (based on the standardized residuals) the bivariate VARMA, GARCH-in-Mean, asymmetric BEKK model does not bear significant misspecification error — see, for example, Kroner and Ng (1998).

In Table 6.3, we also present diagnostic tests suggested by Engle and Ng (1993) and Kroner and Ng (1998), based on the 'generalized residuals,' defined as $e_{i,t}e_{j,t} - h_{ij,t}$ for $i, j = y, o$. For all symmetric GARCH models, the news impact curve — see Engle and Ng (1993) — is symmetric and centered at $e_{i,t-1} = 0$. A generalized residual can be thought of as the distance between a point on the scatter plot of $e_{i,t}e_{j,t}$ from a corresponding point on the news impact curve. If the conditional heteroscedasticity part of the model is correct, $E_{t-1}(e_{i,t}e_{j,t} - h_{ij,t}) = 0$ for all values of i and j, generalized residuals should be uncorrelated with all information known at time $t - 1$. In other words, the unconditional expectation of $e_{i,t}e_{j,t}$ should be equal to its conditional one, $h_{ij,t}$.

The Engle and Ng (1993) and Kroner and Ng (1998) misspecification indicators test whether we can predict the generalized residuals by some variables observed in the past, but which are not included in the model — this is exactly the intuition behind $E_{t-1}(e_{i,t}e_{j,t} - h_{ij,t}) = 0$. In this regard, we follow Kroner and Ng (1998) and Shields *et al.* (2005) and define two sets of misspecification indicators. In a two dimensional space, we first partition $(e_{y,t-1}, e_{o,t-1})$ into four quadrants in terms of the possible sign of the two residuals. Then, to shed light on any possible sign bias of the model, we define the first set of indicator functions as $I(e_{y,t-1} < 0)$, $I(e_{o,t-1} < 0)$, $I(e_{y,t-1} < 0; e_{o,t-1} < 0)$, $I(e_{y,t-1} > 0; e_{o,t-1} < 0)$, $I(e_{y,t-1} < 0; e_{o,t-1} > 0)$ and $I(e_{y,t-1} > 0; e_{o,t-1} > 0)$, where $I(\cdot)$ equals one if the argument is true and zero otherwise. Significance of any of these indicator functions indicates that the model, equations (6.1)-(6.2), is incapable of predicting the effects of some shocks to either y_t or o_t. Moreover, due to the fact that the possible effect of a shock could be a function of both the size and the sign of the shock, we define a second set of indicator functions, $e^2_{y_{t-1}}I(e_{y,t-1} < 0)$, $e^2_{y,t-1}I(e_{o,t-1} < 0)$, $e^2_{o,t-1}I(e_{y,t-1} < 0)$, and $e^2_{o,t-1}I(e_{o,t-1} < 0)$. These indicators are technically scaled versions of the former ones, with the magnitude of the shocks as a scale measure. We conducted indicator tests and report the results in Table 6.3. As can be seen in Table 6.3, most of the indicators fail to reject the null hypothesis of no misspecification — all test statistics in Table 6.3 are distributed as $\chi^2(1)$. Hence, our model, equations (6.1)-(6.2), captures the effects of all sign bias and sign-size scale depended shocks in predicting volatility and there is no significant model misspecification error in the standardized residuals.

Turning now back to Table 6.2, the effect of the conditional volatility in the real price of oil on real GDP growth is given by $\widehat{\psi}_{12}$ in panel A. The point estimate on this coefficient is $-.041$ with a p-value of .000, indicating that the conditional volatility of the real price of oil has a negative effect on the growth rate of real GDP even though Canada is an oil exporting country. We also find that the output growth volatility has a significant negative effect on aggregate economic activity, as it is shown by $\widehat{\psi}_{11}$ in panel A. These findings are consistent with theoretical predictions made in the literature on irreversible investment expenditures and the option value of waiting. They are also consistent with the micro-empirical evidence reported by Kellogg (2010) who provides support for the real options theory by examining how oil companies respond to expected oil price volatility derived from the NYMEX futures options market. In particular, Kellogg (2010) finds that oil firms reduce their drilling activity when expected volatility rises.

We can get a sense of the economic significance of the effect of oil price volatility on output in Canada, by examining the estimated effect of oil price volatility for realistic changes in the conditional standard deviation of the change in the price of oil. We take the sample standard deviation of oil price volatility (which in our model is 29.592) as the average shock to oil price volatility and estimate its effect on output growth by multiplying the effect, -0.041, by the average shock to oil price volatility, 29.592 —

that is, $-0.041 \times 29.592 = -1.213\%$. Hence, an average shock to oil price volatility reduces the growth rate of output by 1.213%, within a quarter. Comparing this effect with the quarterly growth rate of output of 2.659%, we take this effect to be economically significant.

Turning to panel B of Table 6.2, the diagonality restriction, $\gamma_{12}^{(i)} = \gamma_{21}^{(i)} = 0$ for $i = 1, 2$, is rejected, meaning that the data provide strong evidence of the existence of dynamic interactions between y_t and o_t. The null hypothesis of homoscedastic disturbances requires the A, B, and D matrices to be jointly insignificant (that is, $\alpha_{ij} = \beta_{ij} = \delta_{ij} = 0$ for all i, j) and is rejected at the 1% level or better, suggesting that there is significant conditional heteroscedasticity in the data. The null hypothesis of symmetric conditional variance-covariances, which requires all elements of the D matrix to be jointly insignificant (that is, $\delta_{ij} = 0$ for all i, j), is rejected at the 1% level or better, implying the existence of some asymmetries in the data which the model is capable of capturing. Also, the null hypothesis of a diagonal covariance process requires the off-diagonal elements of the A, B, and D matrices to be jointly insignificant (that is, $\alpha_{12} = \alpha_{21} = \beta_{12} = \beta_{21} = \delta_{12} = \delta_{21} = 0$), and is rejected.

Thus the y_t-o_t process is strongly conditionally heteroscedastic, with innovations to oil price changes significantly influencing the conditional variance of output growth in an asymmetric way. Moreover, the sign as well as the size of oil price change innovations are important. In Figures 6.3, 6.4, and 6.5 we plot the conditional standard deviations of output growth and the change in the price of oil as well as the conditional covariance implied by our estimates of the bivariate VARMA, GARCH-in-Mean, asymmetric BEKK model in Table 6.2. In Figure 6.3, output growth volatility coincides with the 1974-75 recession — the biggest recession in the sample. Real GDP growth volatility was also high in 1983:1, 1992:3, and 2009:3. Regarding the change in the real price of oil, o_t, Figure 6.4 shows that the biggest episodes of oil price change volatility took place in 1974, 1981-1982, 1990:1992, and 2008-2009. However, all of these volatility jumps in o_t coincide with recessions. Finally, the conditional covariance between y_t and o_t, shown in Figure 6.5, is highest in 1974:2, followed by 1990:4, 2009:3, and 1986:2.

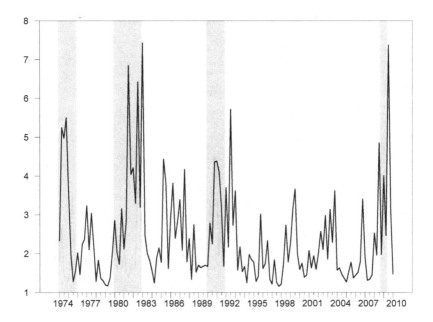

Fig. 6.3 Conditional Standard Deviation of Real Output Growth

6.5   Robustness

We have focused on asymmetries involving the real price of oil as the baseline. This is consistent with most theoretical models of the transmission of oil price shocks that are explicitly based on the real price of oil. Hamilton (2008), however, has made the argument that households and firms may respond to net increases in nominal prices — see also Hamilton (1983, 2003, 2011). Moreover, the use of the real price of oil introduces an additional component of measurement error into our estimated measure of oil price uncertainty, which then captures uncertainty about both the nominal price of oil and the general level of prices (in our case the CPI).

To investigate the robustness of our results, in this section we use the nominal price of oil instead of the real price. In Table 6.4 we report results in the same fashion as those in Table 6.2, based on the nominal oil price. As shown in panel A of the table, the Ljung-Box (1979) Q-statistic cannot reject the null of no autocorrelation for the values and the squared values of the standardized residuals. Also, the failure of the data to reject the null hypotheses of $E(z) = 0$ and $E(z^2) = 1$ indicates that the model with the

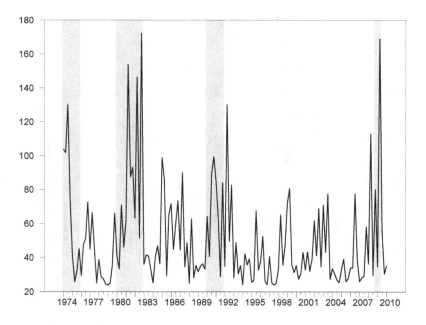

Fig. 6.4   Conditional Standard Deviation of the Change in the Real Price of Oil

nominal price does not bear significant misspecification error. The point estimate on the ψ_{12} coefficient is $-.015$ with a p-value of .000, indicating a comparable effect as that when the real price of oil is used. This is consistent with the arguments made by Hamilton (2008) who notes that "it does not make much difference in summarizing the size of any given shock whether one uses the nominal price or the real price of oil, since in most of these shocks the move in nominal prices is an order of magnitude larger than the change in overall prices during that quarter." Moreover, as can be seen in panel B, the null hypotheses of diagonality, homoscedastic disturbances, symmetric conditional variance-covariances, and a diagonal covariance process are all rejected (as before, when the real price was used).

We also investigate robustness by using higher frequency (monthly) data and the industrial production index as a proxy variable for real output. It is to be noted that industrial output reflects only manufacturing, mining, and utilities, and represents only about 20% of total output. The industrial production index, however, captures economic activity that is likely to be directly affected by oil prices and uncertainty about oil prices. The results for this specification with the real price of oil are reported in Table 6.5 and

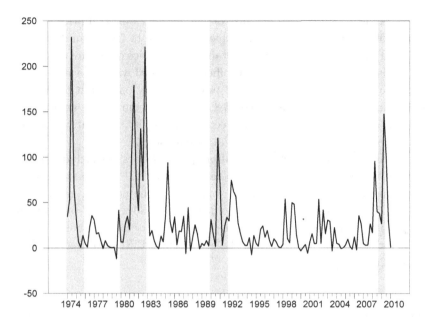

Fig. 6.5   Covariance between Output Growth and the Change in the Real Price of Oil

those with the nominal price of oil in Table 6.6.   Again, the estimate on the
ψ_{12} coefficient is $-.023$ with a p-value of .002 when the real price of oil is
used and $-.023$ with a p-value of .008 when the nominal oil price is used. We
also estimate our model with post-1986 monthly data due to the possibility
of a structural break in the Canadian oil price Energy Program (NEP)
over the period from 1980 to 1985, introduced by the Federal Government
to protect Canadian consumers from the whims of the world oil market.
During this period, the price of oil rose by almost 160%, and the NEP
capped Canadian oil prices at 75% of world oil prices. The results for the
post-1986 period with the nominal price of oil are reported in Table 6.7.
Again, the estimate on the ψ_{12} coefficient indicates the same negative effect
of oil price uncertainty on output growth as that with the full sample.

We further investigate the robustness of our results to alternative measures of the price of oil. In this regard, some researchers believe that the
spot price of WTI oil is not a good proxy for the true global oil market price,
because this oil price variable is influenced by local conditions in Cushing,
Oklahoma. To check the robustness of our results in this regard, we further estimate the model using the U.S. refiner acquisition cost of imported

crude oil as an alternative measure of the nominal world oil price variable. The results with this oil price variable (converted to Canadian dollars and deflated by the Canadian CPI to obtain the real price of oil) are reported in Table 6.8. We find that the ψ_{12} coefficient is $-.003$ with a p-value of .000, indicating the negative effect of oil price volatility on output growth. So our estimates on ψ_{12} in Tables 6.4–6.8 suggest that our results are robust to alternative measures of the level of economic activity, alternative measures of the price of oil, and alternative data frequencies.

Finally, we report results of a subsample that does not include the data for the recent recession. In particular, in Table 6.9 we report results in the same fashion as those in Table 6.2, but for the period from 1974:1 to 2007:3. The estimate on the ψ_{12} coefficient is $-.030$ with a p-value of .000, suggesting that there is less evidence of asymmetry for the shorter sample than for the whole sample, as is the case for the U.S. data used by Kilian (2011, 2012).

6.6 Conclusion

Recent empirical research regarding the relationship between the price of oil and real economic activity has focused on the role of uncertainty about oil prices — see, for example, Chapters 4 and 5. In this chapter, we examine the effects of oil price uncertainty and its asymmetry on real economic activity in Canada, in the context of a bivariate VARMA, GARCH-in-Mean, asymmetric BEKK model. We find that our model embodies a reasonable description of the Canadian data on output growth and the change in the real price of oil. We show that the conditional variance-covariance process underlying output growth and the change in the real price of oil exhibits significant non-diagonality and asymmetry. We also present evidence that increased uncertainty about the change in the real price of oil is associated with a lower average growth rate of real economic activity in Canada, consistent with the results in Chapters 4 and 5 for the United States and Elder and Serletis (2009) for Canada. In this regard, it should be noted that Lee *et al.* (2011) also find (using methods different than ours) that oil price shocks, in interaction with a firm's stock price volatility, have a negative effect on the firm's investment.

Our findings provide an answer to the puzzling asymmetry in the effects of oil price shocks on real activity although the evidence of asymmetries in the conditional variance-covariance matrix does not necessarily translate into asymmetries in the propagation mechanism as argued by Kilian and Vigfusson (2011a,b). That is, plunging oil prices may not boost economic activity, because the sharp rise in the volatility of oil prices may annihilate the good effects of a significant drop in the price of oil. We think that the January 1986 and November 2008 episodes of oil price crashes provide consistent evidence to the asymmetric response of output growth to oil price shocks. In particular, although the January 1986 crash in the oil price was followed by neither a significant increase nor decrease in the growth rate of output, the November 2008 crash that generated a level of oil price uncertainty comparable to that the 1986 crash did, was followed by a significant decrease in the growth rate of real output. It should be noted, however, that although the surge in oil price volatility in the beginning of 1986 and the end of 2008 are similar in magnitude, the causes are different. The former is due to the collapse of OPEC that has nothing to do with the real economy, but the latter is due to the global recession, following the financial crisis. The former is supply driven and nothing happened following the surge, but the latter is a result of shrinking demand. This raises the interesting question of which effect is stronger, the oil price shock effect or the oil price uncertainty effect, and whether the relative strengths of these effects depend on whether the oil price shocks are demand or supply driven. This is an area for potentially productive future research.

Table 6.1 Summary Statistics

A. Summary Statistics

Variable	Mean	Variance	Skewness	Excess kurtosis	J-B normality
y_t	2.650	9.165	-0.533	0.512	8.460 (0.014)
o_t	3.831	3260.445	0.429	9.022	496.301 (0.000)

B. Unit Root and Stationarity Tests

Variable	Unit root tests			KPSS stationarity tests	
	ADF	DF-GLS	Point Optimal Test	$\widehat{\eta}_\mu$	$\widehat{\eta}_\tau$
y_t	-6.662	-5.413	1.939	0.103	0.060
o_t	-10.166	-10.216	11.584	0.140	0.140
5%cv	-3.441	-2.985	5.649	0.463	0.146

C. Engle And Ng (1993) Tests For Sign and Size Bias In Variance

Variable	Sign	Negative size	Positive size	Join
y_t	11.565 (.331)	-.495 (.000)	.047 (.691)	18.420 (.000)
o_t	2077.077 (.111)	-64.934 (.000)	4.794 (.707)	30.384 (.000)

Note: Numbers in parentheses are tail areas of tests.

Table 6.2   The Bivariate VARMA, GARCH-in-Mean,
Asymmetric BEKK Model with Quarterly Real GDP Data
and the Real Price of Oil

Equations (6.1) and (6.2) with $p = q = 2$ and $f = g = 1$

A. Conditional mean equation

$$a = \begin{bmatrix} 2.751 \\ (0.000) \\ -9.183 \\ (0.014) \end{bmatrix} ; \Gamma_1 = \begin{bmatrix} 1.443 & 0.175 \\ (0.000) & (0.000) \\ 0.391 & -0.281 \\ (0.673) & (0.000) \end{bmatrix} ; \Gamma_2 = \begin{bmatrix} -0.608 & 0.077 \\ (0.000) & (0.000) \\ -0.709 & -0.100 \\ (0.053) & (0.034) \end{bmatrix} ;$$

$$\Theta_1 = \begin{bmatrix} -1.015 & -0.173 \\ (0.000) & (0.000) \\ 3.003 & 0.597 \\ (0.028) & (0.000) \end{bmatrix} ; \Theta_2 = \begin{bmatrix} -0.699 & -0.139 \\ (0.000) & (0.000) \\ 2.168 & 0.094 \\ (0.000) & (0.107) \end{bmatrix} ; \Psi_1 = \begin{bmatrix} -1.084 & -0.041 \\ (0.000) & (0.000) \\ -1.829 & 0.547 \\ (0.183) & (0.000) \end{bmatrix} .$$

Residual diagnostics

	Mean	Variance	$Q(4)$	$Q^2(4)$	$Q(12)$	$Q^2(12)$
z_{y_t}	0.084	1.275	5.649	1.946	13.588	10.825
			(0.226)	(0.745)	(0.327)	(0.543)
z_{o_t}	-0.039	0.730	2.771	2.934	13.542	6.705
			(0.596)	(0.568)	(0.330)	(0.876)

Note: Sample period, quarterly data: 1974:1-2010:1.
Numbers in parentheses are tail areas of tests.

Table 6.2 cont'd

B. Conditional variance-covariance structure

$$C = \begin{bmatrix} 0.186 & -15.873 \\ (0.681) & (0.028) \\ & -17.297 \\ & (0.000) \end{bmatrix} ; B = \begin{bmatrix} 0.343 & 1.400 \\ (0.104) & (0.335) \\ -0.045 & -0.092 \\ (0.000) & (0.000) \end{bmatrix} ;$$

$$A = \begin{bmatrix} 0.057 & 19.792 \\ (0.642) & (0.000) \\ -0.008 & -0.274 \\ (0.080) & (0.001) \end{bmatrix} ; D = \begin{bmatrix} -0.189 & -6.686 \\ (0.135) & (0.264) \\ -0.003 & 0.326 \\ (0.520) & (0.004) \end{bmatrix} .$$

Hypotheses testing

Diagonal VARMA	$H_0 : \gamma_{12}^{(i)} = \gamma_{21}^{(i)} = \theta_{12}^{(l)} = \theta_{21}^{(l)} = 0$, for $i, l = 1, 2$	0.000
No GARCH	$H_0 : \alpha_{ij} = \beta_{ij} = \delta_{ij} = 0$, for all i, j	0.000
No GARCH-M	$H_0 : \psi_{ij} = 0$, for all i, j	0.000
No asymmetry	$H_0 : \delta_{ij} = 0$, for $i, j = 1, 2$	0.004
Diagonal GARCH	$H_0 : \alpha_{12} = \alpha_{21} = \beta_{12} = \beta_{21} = \delta_{12} = \delta_{21} = 0$	0.000

Note: Sample period, quarterly data: 1974:1-2010:1.
Numbers in parentheses are tail areas of tests.

Table 6.3 Diagnostic Tests Based on the News Impact Curve

	$\varepsilon_{y,t}^2 - h_{yy,t}$	$\varepsilon_{y,t}\varepsilon_{o,t} - h_{yo,t}$	$\varepsilon_{o,t}^2 - h_{oo,t}$
$I(e_{y,t-1} < 0)$	1.369 (0.241)	0.038 (0.845)	1.246 (0.264)
$I(e_{o,t-1} < 0)$	0.510 (0.475)	0.124 (0.724)	0.067 (0.794)
$I(e_{y,t-1} < 0, e_{o,t-1} < 0)$	0.197 (0.656)	0.023 (0.879)	7.992 (0.004)
$I(e_{y,t-1} > 0, e_{o,t-1} < 0)$	0.068 (0.793)	1.451 (0.228)	0.301 (0.583)
$I(e_{y,t-1} < 0, e_{o,t-1} > 0)$	0.730 (0.392)	0.113 (0.736)	0.304 (0.580)
$I(e_{y,t-1} > 0, e_{o,t-1} > 0)$	0.041 (0.838)	1.083 (0.297)	1.083 (0.297)
$e_{y,t-1}^2 I(e_{y,t-1} < 0)$	0.401 (0.526)	0.208 (0.647)	0.010 (0.917)
$e_{y,t-1}^2 I(e_{o,t-1} < 0)$	0.033 (0.854)	0.003 (0.953)	0.039 (0.842)
$e_{o,t-1}^2 I(e_{y,t-1} < 0)$	0.557 (0.455)	0.063 (0.800)	1.559 (0.211)
$e_{o,t-1}^2 I(e_{o,t-1} < 0)$	2.168 (0.140)	0.026 (0.871)	2.034 (0.153)

Note: Numbers in parentheses are tail areas of tests.

Table 6.4 The Bivariate VARMA, GARCH-in-Mean,
Asymmetric BEKK Model with Quarterly Real GDP Data
and the Nominal Price of Oil

Equations (6.1) and (6.2) with $p = q = 2$ and $f = g = 1$

A. Conditional mean equation

$$
\mathbf{a} = \begin{bmatrix} 0.218 \\ (0.798) \\ -6.168 \\ (0.000) \end{bmatrix} ; \boldsymbol{\Gamma}_1 = \begin{bmatrix} 0.117 & -0.008 \\ (0.520) & (0.385) \\ 2.651 & 0.736 \\ (0.000) & (0.000) \end{bmatrix} ; \boldsymbol{\Gamma}_2 = \begin{bmatrix} 0.352 & 0.029 \\ (0.056) & (0.040) \\ -2.679 & 0.216 \\ (0.000) & (0.000) \end{bmatrix} ;
$$

$$
\boldsymbol{\Theta}_1 = \begin{bmatrix} 0.455 & 0.010 \\ (0.020) & (0.248) \\ -2.757 & -0.489 \\ (0.000) & (0.000) \end{bmatrix} ; \boldsymbol{\Theta}_2 = \begin{bmatrix} -0.190 & -0.028 \\ (0.125) & (0.054) \\ 0.627 & -0.473 \\ (0.123) & (0.000) \end{bmatrix} ; \boldsymbol{\Psi}_1 = \begin{bmatrix} 0.779 & -0.015 \\ (0.000) & (0.000) \\ -0.407 & 0.115 \\ (0.370) & (0.000) \end{bmatrix}
$$

Residual diagnostics

	Mean	Variance	$Q(4)$	$Q^2(4)$	$Q(12)$	$Q^2(12)$
z_{yt}	0.108	1.097	1.015	13.548	12.887	33.034
			(0.907)	(0.008)	(0.377)	(0.001)
z_{ot}	0.150	0.759	6.580	4.335	19.353	10.151
			(0.159)	(0.362)	(0.080)	(0.602)

Note: Sample period, quarterly data: 1971:1-2010:1.
Numbers in parentheses are tail areas of tests.

Table 6.4 cont'd

B. Conditional variance-covariance structure

$$C = \begin{bmatrix} 0.639 & -1.318 \\ (0.000) & (0.059) \\ & -0.001 \\ & (0.999) \end{bmatrix} ; B = \begin{bmatrix} -0.836 & 2.894 \\ (0.000) & (0.000) \\ 0.020 & 0.496 \\ (0.000) & (0.000) \end{bmatrix} ;$$

$$A = \begin{bmatrix} -0.061 & 0.298 \\ (0.665) & (0.674) \\ 0.011 & 0.815 \\ (0.215) & (0.000) \end{bmatrix} ; D = \begin{bmatrix} -0.559 & 1.533 \\ (0.000) & (0.030) \\ 0.014 & 1.335 \\ (0.307) & (0.003) \end{bmatrix}$$

Hypotheses testing

Diagonal VARMA	$H_0 : \gamma_{12}^{(i)} = \gamma_{21}^{(i)} = \theta_{12}^{(l)} = \theta_{21}^{(l)} = 0$, for $i, l = 1, 2$	0.000
No GARCH	$H_0 : \alpha_{ij} = \beta_{ij} = \delta_{ij} = 0$, for all i, j	0.000
No GARCH-M	$H_0 : \psi_{ij} = 0$, for all i, j	0.000
No asymmetry	$H_0 : \delta_{ij} = 0$, for $i, j = 1, 2$	0.000
Diagonal GARCH	$H_0 : \alpha_{12} = \alpha_{21} = \beta_{12} = \beta_{21} = \delta_{12} = \delta_{21} = 0$	0.000

Note: Sample period, quarterly data: 1971:1-2010:1.
Numbers in parentheses are tail areas of tests.

Table 6.5 The Bivariate VARMA, GARCH-in-Mean,
Asymmetric BEKK Model with Monthly IPI Data
and the Real Price of Oil

Equations (6.1) and (6.2) with $p = q = 2$ and $f = g = 1$

A. Conditional mean equation

$$
a = \begin{bmatrix} 2.476 \\ (0.001) \\ -2.074 \\ (0.560) \end{bmatrix} ; \Gamma_1 = \begin{bmatrix} 0.794 & -0.004 \\ (0.000) & (0.519) \\ 0.262 & 1.184 \\ (0.755) & (0.000) \end{bmatrix} ; \Gamma_2 = \begin{bmatrix} 0.001 & 0.032 \\ (0.994) & (0.000) \\ 0.128 & -0.283 \\ (0.885) & (0.052) \end{bmatrix} ;
$$

$$
\Theta_1 = \begin{bmatrix} -0.933 & 0.010 \\ (0.000) & (0.156) \\ 0.324 & -1.015 \\ (0.668) & (0.000) \end{bmatrix} ; \Theta_2 = \begin{bmatrix} 0.256 & -0.040 \\ (0.108) & (0.000) \\ 0.012 & 0.087 \\ (0.986) & (0.597) \end{bmatrix} ; \Psi_1 = \begin{bmatrix} 0.002 & -0.023 \\ (0.941) & (0.002) \\ -0.067 & 0.036 \\ (0.141) & (0.355) \end{bmatrix} .
$$

Residual diagnostics

	Mean	Variance	$Q(4)$	$Q^2(4)$	$Q(12)$	$Q^2(12)$
z_{yt}	0.068	1.041	5.184	4.903	23.242	21.462
			(0.268)	(0.297)	(0.025)	(0.043)
z_{ot}	-0.012	0.730	1.330	0.001	6.425	0.281
			(0.856)	(0.999)	(0.893)	(0.999)

Note: Sample period, monthly data: 1974:1-2010:1.
Numbers in parentheses are tail areas of tests.

Table 6.5 cont'd

B. Conditional variance-covariance structure

$$C = \begin{bmatrix} 0.315 & 38.865 \\ (0.619) & (0.030) \\ & 77.095 \\ & (0.000) \end{bmatrix} ; \; B = \begin{bmatrix} 0.935 & 0.038 \\ (0.000) & (0.864) \\ -0.010 & 0.001 \\ (0.000) & (0.985) \end{bmatrix} ;$$

$$A = \begin{bmatrix} -0.044 & 0.030 \\ (0.687) & (0.903) \\ 0.006 & 0.521 \\ (0.018) & (0.000) \end{bmatrix} ; \; D = \begin{bmatrix} 0.509 & 0.085 \\ (0.000) & (0.640) \\ 0.004 & 0.060 \\ (0.183) & (0.299) \end{bmatrix} .$$

Hypotheses testing

Diagonal VARMA	$H_0 : \gamma_{12}^{(i)} = \gamma_{21}^{(i)} = \theta_{12}^{(l)} = \theta_{21}^{(l)} = 0$, for $i, l = 1, 2$	0.000
No GARCH	$H_0 : \alpha_{ij} = \beta_{ij} = \delta_{ij} = 0$, for all i, j	0.000
No GARCH-M	$H_0 : \psi_{ij} = 0$, for all i, j	0.000
No asymmetry	$H_0 : \delta_{ij} = 0$, for $i, j = 1, 2$	0.000
Diagonal GARCH	$H_0 : \alpha_{12} = \alpha_{21} = \beta_{12} = \beta_{21} = \delta_{12} = \delta_{21} = 0$	0.102

Note: Sample period, monthly data: 1974:1-2010:1.
Numbers in parentheses are tail areas of tests.

118

Oil Price Uncertainty

Table 6.6 The Bivariate VARMA, GARCH-in-Mean,
Asymmetric BEKK Model with Monthly IPI Data
and the Nominal Price of Oil

Equations (6.1) and (6.2) with $p = q = 2$, and $f = g = 1$

A. Conditional mean equation

$$
\mathbf{a} = \begin{bmatrix} 5.642 \\ (0.012) \\ 34.223 \\ (0.213) \end{bmatrix} ; \mathbf{\Gamma}_1 = \begin{bmatrix} -0.102 & 0.004 \\ (0.070) & (0.207) \\ 0.064 & 0.187 \\ (0.856) & (0.000) \end{bmatrix} ; \mathbf{\Gamma}_2 = \begin{bmatrix} 0.190 & -0.002 \\ (0.000) & (0.326) \\ 0.265 & -0.077 \\ (0.410) & (0.149) \end{bmatrix} ;
$$

$$
\mathbf{\Theta}_1 = \begin{bmatrix} -0.115 & -0.016 \\ (0.856) & (0.342) \\ 1.366 & 0.202 \\ (0.538) & (0.143) \end{bmatrix} ; \mathbf{\Theta}_2 = \begin{bmatrix} 0.211 & 0.001 \\ (0.000) & (0.922) \\ 0.331 & 0.002 \\ (0.296) & (0.956) \end{bmatrix} ; \mathbf{\Psi} = \begin{bmatrix} 0.100 & -0.023 \\ (0.874) & (0.008) \\ -1.772 & -0.425 \\ (0.450) & (0.125) \end{bmatrix}
$$

Residual diagnostics

	Mean	Variance	$Q(4)$	$Q^2(4)$	$Q(12)$	$Q^2(12)$
z_{yt}	0.024	1.021	2.590	4.861	21.246	18.620
			(0.628)	(0.301)	(0.046)	(0.098)
z_{ot}	-0.033	0.747	11.418	1.998	15.239	19.651
			(0.022)	(0.736)	(0.228)	(0.073)

Note: Sample period, monthly data: 1974:1-2010:1.
Numbers in parentheses are tail areas of tests.

Table 6.6 cont'd

B. Conditional variance-covariance structure

$$
C = \begin{bmatrix} 0.222 & 86.934 \\ (0.525) & (0.000) \\ & 0.001 \\ & (0.999) \end{bmatrix} ; \;
B = \begin{bmatrix} 0.939 & -0.054 \\ (0.000) & (0.804) \\ -0.011 & 0.033 \\ (0.000) & (0.713) \end{bmatrix} ;
$$

$$
A = \begin{bmatrix} 0.124 & 0.077 \\ (0.550) & (0.736) \\ 0.006 & 0.534 \\ (0.063) & (0.008) \end{bmatrix} ; \;
D = \begin{bmatrix} 0.445 & 0.051 \\ (0.000) & (0.775) \\ 0.007 & 0.029 \\ (0.033) & (0.641) \end{bmatrix} .
$$

Hypotheses testing

Diagonal VARMA	$H_0 : \gamma_{12}^{(i)} = \gamma_{21}^{(i)} = \theta_{12}^{(l)} = \theta_{21}^{(l)} = 0$, for $i, l = 1, 2$	0.517
No GARCH	$H_0 : \alpha_{ij} = \beta_{ij} = \delta_{ij} = 0$, for all i, j	0.000
No GARCH-M	$H_0 : \psi_{ij} = 0$, for all $i, j = 1, 2$	0.001
No asymmetry	$H_0 : \delta_{ij} = 0$, for $i, j = 1, 2$	0.000
Diagonal GARCH	$H_0 : \alpha_{12} = \alpha_{21} = \beta_{12} = \beta_{21} = \delta_{12} = \delta_{21} = 0$	0.001

Note: Sample period, monthly data: 1974:1-2010:1.
Numbers in parentheses are tail areas of tests.

Table 6.7   The Bivariate VARMA, GARCH-in-Mean,
Asymmetric BEKK Model with Monthly IPI Data and
the Nominal Price of Oil (Post 1986 Period)

Equations (6.1) and (6.2) with $p = q = 2$, and $f = g = 1$

A. Conditional mean equation

$$
\mathbf{a} = \begin{bmatrix} 3.642 \\ (0.041) \\ -4.390 \\ (0.891) \end{bmatrix} ; \mathbf{\Gamma}_1 = \begin{bmatrix} -0.040 & 0.006 \\ (0.522) & (0.100) \\ 0.174 & 0.178 \\ (0.863) & (0.001) \end{bmatrix} ; \mathbf{\Gamma}_2 = \begin{bmatrix} 0.154 & -0.003 \\ (0.005) & (0.176) \\ 0.107 & -0.062 \\ (0.890) & (0.197) \end{bmatrix} ;
$$

$$
\mathbf{\Theta}_1 = \begin{bmatrix} -3.527 & 0.026 \\ (0.008) & (0.283) \\ 78.310 & 0.257 \\ (0.223) & (0.475) \end{bmatrix} ; \mathbf{\Theta}_2 = \begin{bmatrix} 0.261 & 0.002 \\ (0.000) & (0.475) \\ -0.255 & 0.036 \\ (0.705) & (0.488) \end{bmatrix} ; \mathbf{\Psi} = \begin{bmatrix} 3.607 & -0.053 \\ (0.008) & (0.053) \\ -80.418 & -0.032 \\ (0.216) & (0.934) \end{bmatrix} .
$$

Residual diagnostics

	Mean	Variance	$Q(4)$	$Q^2(4)$	$Q(12)$	$Q^2(12)$
z_{yt}	0.033	1.322	0.389	0.866	7.200	14.257
			(0.983)	(0.929)	(0.844)	(0.284)
z_{ot}	-0.001	0.821	1.350	3.894	7.959	8.568
			(0.852)	(0.420)	(0.788)	(0.739)

Note: Sample period, monthly data: 1986:1-2010:1.
Numbers in parentheses are tail areas of tests.

Table 6.7 cont'd

B. Conditional variance-covariance structure

$$C = \begin{bmatrix} 0.107 & -34.567 \\ (0.741) & (0.206) \\ & -22.988 \\ & (0.565) \end{bmatrix} ; B = \begin{bmatrix} 0.975 & -0.538 \\ (0.000) & (0.734) \\ -0.015 & -0.727 \\ (0.009) & (0.000) \end{bmatrix} ;$$

$$A = \begin{bmatrix} 0.045 & -0.390 \\ (0.209) & (0.722) \\ 0.005 & 0.521 \\ (0.030) & (0.000) \end{bmatrix} ; D = \begin{bmatrix} 0.187 & -1.294 \\ (0.061) & (0.310) \\ 0.002 & 0.153 \\ (0.313) & (0.257) \end{bmatrix} .$$

Hypotheses testing

Diagonal VARMA	$H_0 : \gamma_{12}^{(i)} = \gamma_{21}^{(i)} = \theta_{12}^{(l)} = \theta_{21}^{(l)} = 0$, for $i, l = 1, 2$	0.306
No GARCH	$H_0 : \alpha_{ij} = \beta_{ij} = \delta_{ij} = 0$, for all i, j	0.000
No GARCH-M	$H_0 : \psi_{ij} = 0$, for all $i, j = 1, 2$	0.029
No asymmetry	$H_0 : \delta_{ij} = 0$, for $i, j = 1, 2$	0.122
Diagonal GARCH	$H_0 : \alpha_{12} = \alpha_{21} = \beta_{12} = \beta_{21} = \delta_{12} = \delta_{21} = 0$	0.011

Note: Sample period, monthly data: 1986:1-2010:1.
Numbers in parentheses are tail areas of tests.

Table 6.8 The Bivariate VARMA, GARCH-in-Mean,
Asymmetric BEKK Model with Monthly IPI Data and
the Real Price of Oil Based on the Acquisition Cost

Equations (6.1) and (6.2) with $p = q = 2$, and $f = g = 1$

A. Conditional mean equation

$$
a = \begin{bmatrix} 0.774 \\ (0.000) \\ -0.299 \\ (0.173) \end{bmatrix} ;
\Gamma_1 = \begin{bmatrix} 0.793 & -0.002 \\ (0.000) & (0.709) \\ 0.202 & 1.295 \\ (0.002) & (0.000) \end{bmatrix} ;
\Gamma_2 = \begin{bmatrix} 0.004 & 0.014 \\ (0.964) & (0.011) \\ 0.285 & -0.379 \\ (0.001) & (0.000) \end{bmatrix} ;
$$

$$
\Theta_1 = \begin{bmatrix} -0.922 & 0.010 \\ (0.000) & (0.128) \\ -0.190 & 0.875 \\ (0.235) & (0.000) \end{bmatrix} ;
\Theta_2 = \begin{bmatrix} 0.241 & -0.022 \\ (0.006) & (0.000) \\ -0.336 & -0.067 \\ (0.047) & (0.451) \end{bmatrix} ;
\Psi = \begin{bmatrix} -0.011 & -0.003 \\ (0.081) & (0.000) \\ -0.015 & -0.005 \\ (0.045) & (0.118) \end{bmatrix}
$$

Residual diagnostics

	Mean	Variance	$Q(4)$	$Q^2(4)$	$Q(12)$	$Q^2(12)$
z_{yt}	-0.002	1.009	4.289	4.947	23.002	20.356
			(0.368)	(0.292)	(0.027)	(0.060)
z_{ot}	-0.041	0.984	3.156	1.389	11.471	3.932
			(0.532)	(0.846)	(0.489)	(0.984)

Note: Sample period, monthly data: 1974:1-2010:1.
Numbers in parentheses are tail areas of tests.

Table 6.8 cont'd

B. Conditional variance-covariance structure

$$C = \begin{bmatrix} -0.760 & 9.709 \\ (0.010) & (0.395) \\ & 10.064 \\ & (0.419) \end{bmatrix} ; B = \begin{bmatrix} 0.938 & 0.016 \\ (0.000) & (0.746) \\ -0.001 & 0.790 \\ (0.185) & (0.000) \end{bmatrix} ;$$

$$A = \begin{bmatrix} 0.029 & 0.135 \\ (0.567) & (0.201) \\ -0.006 & -0.683 \\ (0.033) & (0.000) \end{bmatrix} ; D = \begin{bmatrix} 0.488 & -0.004 \\ (0.000) & (0.968) \\ 0.004 & -0.063 \\ (0.059) & (0.407) \end{bmatrix} .$$

Hypotheses testing

Diagonal VARMA	$H_0 : \gamma_{12}^{(i)} = \gamma_{21}^{(i)} = \theta_{12}^{(l)} = \theta_{21}^{(l)} = 0$, for $i, l = 1, 2$	0.000
No GARCH	$H_0 : \alpha_{ij} = \beta_{ij} = \delta_{ij} = 0$, for all i, j	0.000
No GARCH-M	$H_0 : \psi_{ij} = 0$, for all $i, j = 1, 2$	0.000
No asymmetry	$H_0 : \delta_{ij} = 0$, for $i, j = 1, 2$	0.000
Diagonal GARCH	$H_0 : \alpha_{12} = \alpha_{21} = \beta_{12} = \beta_{21} = \delta_{12} = \delta_{21} = 0$	0.310

Note: Sample period, monthly data: 1974:1-2010:1.
Numbers in parentheses are tail areas of tests.

Table 6.9 The Bivariate VARMA, GARCH-in-Mean,
Asymmetric BEKK Model with Quarterly Real GDP Data
and the Real Price of Oil
(for the Period Excluding the Recent Recession)

Equations (6.1) and (6.2) with $p = q = 2$ and $f = g = 1$

A. Conditional mean equation

$$
\mathbf{a} = \begin{bmatrix} -0.567 \\ (0.154) \\ 3.130 \\ (0.029) \end{bmatrix} ; \boldsymbol{\Gamma}_1 = \begin{bmatrix} 1.650 & 0.479 \\ (0.000) & (0.000) \\ 1.188 & -0.826 \\ (0.023) & (0.000) \end{bmatrix} ; \boldsymbol{\Gamma}_2 = \begin{bmatrix} -1.576 & 0.310 \\ (0.000) & (0.000) \\ 0.728 & -0.265 \\ (0.003) & (0.000) \end{bmatrix} ;
$$

$$
\boldsymbol{\Theta}_1 = \begin{bmatrix} -1.091 & -0.487 \\ (0.000) & (0.000) \\ 0.894 & 1.035 \\ (0.211) & (0.000) \end{bmatrix} ; \boldsymbol{\Theta}_2 = \begin{bmatrix} -0.376 & -0.400 \\ (0.045) & (0.000) \\ 1.023 & 0.311 \\ (0.000) & (0.000) \end{bmatrix} ; \boldsymbol{\Psi}_1 = \begin{bmatrix} -0.394 & -0.030 \\ (0.089) & (0.000) \\ -0.241 & 0.135 \\ (0.653) & (0.000) \end{bmatrix}
$$

Residual diagnostics

	Mean	Variance	$Q(4)$	$Q^2(4)$	$Q(12)$	$Q^2(12)$
z_{yt}	0.071	1.280	2.137	1.869	9.768	10.633
			(0.710)	(0.759)	(0.636)	(0.560)
z_{ot}	-0.066	0.832	1.312	0.375	13.307	4.382
			(0.859)	(0.984)	(0.347)	(0.975)

Note: Sample period, quarterly data: 1974:1–2007:3.
Numbers in parentheses are tail areas of tests.

Table 6.9 cont'd

B. Conditional variance-covariance structure

$$C = \begin{bmatrix} -0.125 & -29.465 \\ (0.662) & (0.000) \\ & -1.867 \\ & (0.947) \end{bmatrix} ; \; B = \begin{bmatrix} -0.067 & -0.084 \\ (0.389) & (0.829) \\ 0.041 & 0.055 \\ (0.000) & (0.475) \end{bmatrix} ;$$

$$A = \begin{bmatrix} 0.138 & 20.352 \\ (0.093) & (0.000) \\ -0.014 & -0.254 \\ (0.000) & (0.000) \end{bmatrix} ; \; D = \begin{bmatrix} -0.005 & 0.390 \\ (0.541) & (0.622) \\ -0.003 & 0.149 \\ (0.418) & (0.080) \end{bmatrix} .$$

Hypotheses testing

Diagonal VARMA	$H_0 : \gamma_{12}^{(i)} = \gamma_{21}^{(i)} = \theta_{12}^{(l)} = \theta_{21}^{(l)} = 0$, for $i, l = 1, 2$	0.000
No GARCH	$H_0 : \alpha_{ij} = \beta_{ij} = \delta_{ij} = 0$, for all i, j	0.000
No GARCH-M	$H_0 : \psi_{ij} = 0$, for all i, j	0.000
No asymmetry	$H_0 : \delta_{ij} = 0$, for $i, j = 1, 2$	0.387
Diagonal GARCH	$H_0 : \alpha_{12} = \alpha_{21} = \beta_{12} = \beta_{21} = \delta_{12} = \delta_{21} = 0$	0.000

Note: Sample period, quarterly data: 1974:1-2007:3.
Numbers in parentheses are tail areas of tests.

Bibliography

Alquist, R., L. Kilian, and R. Vigfusson. "Forecasting the Price of Oil." In *Handbook of Economic Forecasting* (2011, forthcoming).

Andersen, T.G., T. Bollerslev, P.F. Christoffersen, and F.X. Diebold. "Volatility and Correlation Forecasting." In G. Elliot, C.W.J. Granger, and A. Timmermann (Eds.), *Handbook of Economic Forecasting*. Amsterdam: North-Holland (2006), 778-878.

Aguerrevere, F. "Real Options, Product Market Competition and Asset Returns." *Journal of Finance* 64 (2009), 957-983.

Bauwens, L., S. Laurent, and J.V.K. Rombouts. "Multivariate GARCH Models: A Survey." *Journal of Applied Econometrics* 21 (2006), 79-109.

Bernanke, B.S. "Irreversibility, Uncertainty, and Cyclical Investment." *Quarterly Journal of Economics* 98 (1983), 85-106.

Bernanke, B.S., M. Gertler, and M. Watson. "Systematic Monetary Policy and the Effects of Oil Price Shocks." *Brookings Papers on Economic Activity* 1 (1997), 91-142.

Black, F. and M. Scholes. "The Pricing of Options and Corporate Liabilities." *Journal of Political Economy* 81 (1973), 637-654.

Blanchard, O.J. and J. Galí. "The Macroeconomic Effects of Oil Price Shocks: Why Are the 2000s So Different from the 1970s?" In J. Gali and M. Gertler (Eds.), *International Dimensions of Monetary Policy*. Chicago: University of Chicago Press (2010), 373-421.

Blanchard, O.J. and M. Riggi. "Why Are the 2000s So Different from the 1970s? A Structural Interpretation of Changes in the Macroeconomic Effects of Oil Prices." Working Paper No. 15467 (2009), NBER, Cambridge, MA.

Bollerslev, T. "Generalized Autoregressive Conditional Heteroscedasticity." *Journal of Econometrics* 31 (1986), 307-27.

Bollerslev, T. "Modeling the Coherence in Short-Term Nominal Exchange Rates: A Multivariate Generalized ARCH Approach." *Review of Economics and Statistics* 72 (1990), 498-505.

Bollerslev, T., R.Y. Chou, and K.F. Kroner. "ARCH Modeling in Finance: A Review of the Theory and Empirical Evidence." *Journal of Econometrics* 52 (1992), 5-59.

Bollerslev, T., R.F. Engle, and D.B. Nelson. "ARCH Models." In R.F. Engle and D.L. McFadden (Eds.) *Handbook of Econometrics*, Vol. 4. Amsterdam: Elsevier (1994).

Bollerslev, T., R.F. Engle, and J. Wooldridge. "A Capital Asset Pricing Model with Time-Varying Covariances." *Journal of Political Economy* 96 (1988), 116-131.

Brennan, M. "Latent Assets." *Journal of Finance* 45 (1990), 709-730.

Brennan, M. and E. Schwartz. "Evaluating Natural Resource Investment." *Journal of Business* 58 (1985), 1135-1157.

Campbell, J.Y., A.W. Lo, and A.C. MacKinlay. *The Econometrics of Financial Markets*. Princeton: Princeton University Press (1997).

Cushman, D.O. and T. Zha. "Identifying Monetary Policy in a Small Open Economy under Flexible Exchange Rates." *Journal of Monetary Economics* 39 (1997), 433-448.

Davis, S.J. "Allocative Disturbances and Specific Capital in Real Business Cycle Theories." *American Economic Review Papers and Proceedings* 77 (1987), 738-751.

Davis, S.J. and J. Haltiwanger. "Sectoral Job Creation and Destruction Responses to Oil Price Changes." *Journal of Monetary Economics* 48 (2001), 465-512.

Dickey, D.A., and W.A. Fuller. "Likelihood Ratio Statistics for Autoregressive Time Series with a Unit Root." *Econometrica* 49 (1981), 1057-72.

Ding, Z., C.W.J. Granger, and R.F. Engle. "A Long Memory Property of Stock Market Returns and a New Model." *Journal of Empirical Finance* 1 (1993), 83-106.

Edelstein, P. and L. Kilian. "The Response of Business Fixed Investment to Changes in Energy Prices: A Test of Some Hypotheses about the Transmission of Energy Price Shocks." *The B.E. Journal of Macroeconomics* (Contributions) 7 (2007), Article 35.

Edelstein, P. and L. Kilian. "How Sensitive are Consumer Expenditures to Retail Energy Prices?" *Journal of Monetary Economics* 56 (2009), 766-779.

Elder, J. Macroeconomic and Financial Effects of Monetary Policy and Monetary Policy Uncertainty. Ph.D. Dissertation, University of Virginia (1995).

Elder, J. "An Impulse-Response-Function for a Vector Autoregression with Multivariate GARCH-in-Mean." *Economics Letters* 79 (2003), 21 26.

Elder, J. "Another Perspective on the Effects of Inflation Volatility." *Journal of Money, Credit and Banking* 36 (2004), 911-28.

Elder, J. and A. Serletis. "Oil Price Uncertainty in Canada." *Energy Economics* 31 (2009), 852-856.

Elder, J. and A. Serletis. "Oil Price Uncertainty." *Journal of Money, Credit and Banking* 42 (2010), 1137-1159.

Elder, J. and A. Serletis. "Volatility in Oil Prices and Manufacturing Activity: An Investigation of Real Options." *Macroeconomic Dynamics* 15 (Supplement 3) (2011), 379-395.

Elliot, G., T.J. Rothenberg, and J.H. Stock. "Efficient Tests for an Autoregressive Unit Root." *Econometrica* 64 (1996), 813-836.

Engle, R.F. "Autoregressive Conditional Heteroscedasticity with Estimates of the Variance of U.K. Inflation." *Econometrica* 50 (1982), 987–1008.

Engle, R.F. "Dynamic Conditional Correlation: A Simple Class of Multivariate GARCH Models." *Journal of Business and Economic Statistics* 20 (2002), 339-350.

Engle, R.F. and C.W.J. Granger. "Cointegration and Error Correction: Representation, Estimation and Testing." *Econometrica* 55 (1987), 251-276.

Engle, R.F. and K.F. Kroner. "Multivariate Simultaneous Generalized ARCH." *Econometric Theory* 11 (1995), 122-150.

Engle, R.F. and V.K. Ng. "Measuring and Testing the Impact of News on Volatility." *Journal of Finance* 5 (1993), 1749-1778.

Engle, R.F., D.M. Lilien, and R.P. Robins. "Estimating Time Varying Risk Premia in the Term Structure." *Econometrica* 55 (1987), 391-407.

Engle, R.F., V.K. Ng, and M. Rothschild. "Asset Pricing with a Factor-Arch Covariance Structure: Empirical Estimates for Treasury Bills." *Journal of Econometrics* 45 (1990), 213-237.

Ferderer, J.P. "Oil Price Volatility and the Macroeconomy." *Journal of Macroeconomics* 18 (1996), 1-26.

Finn, M.G. "Perfect Competition and the Effects of Energy Price Increases on Economic Activity." *Journal of Money, Credit, and Banking* 32 (2000), 400-416.

Gibson, R. and E.S. Schwartz. "Stochastic Convenience Yield and the Pricing of Oil Contingent Claims." *Journal of Finance* 45 (1990), 959-976.

Glosten, L.R., R. Jaganathan, and D. Runkle. "On the Relation between the Expected Value and the Volatility of the Normal Excess Return on Stocks." *Journal of Finance* 48 (1993), 1779-1801.

Grier, K.B., Ó.T. Henry, N. Olekalns, and K. Shields. "The Asymmetric Effects of Uncertainty on Inflation and Output Growth." *Journal of Applied Econometrics* 19 (2004), 551-565.

Hafner, C.M. and H. Herwartz. "Volatility Impulse Response Functions for Multivariate GARCH Models: An Exchange Rate Illustration." *Journal of International Money and Finance* 25 (2006), 719-740.

Hamilton, J.D. "Oil and the Macroeconomy since World War II." *Journal of Political Economy* 91 (1983), 228-248.

Hamilton, J.D. "A Neoclassical Model of Unemployment and the Business Cycle." *Journal of Political Economy* 96 (1988), 593-617.

Hamilton, J.D. *Time Series Analysis.* Princeton: Princeton University Press (1994).

Hamilton, J.D. "This is What Happened to the Oil Price-Macroeconomy Relationship." *Journal of Monetary Economics* 38 (1996), 215-220.

Hamilton, J.D. "What is an Oil Shock?" *Journal of Econometrics* 113 (2003), 363-398.

Hamilton, J.D. "Oil and the Macroeconomy." In Durlauf, S.N. and L.E. Blume (Eds.). *The New Palgrave Dictionary of Economics.* Palgrave Macmillan (2008).

Hamilton, J.D. "Causes and Consequences of the Oil Shock of 2007-08." *Brookings Papers on Economic Activity* (2009), 215-259.

Hamilton, J.D. "Nonlinearities and the Macroeconomic Effects of Oil Prices." *Macroeconomic Dynamics* 15 (Supplement 3) (2011), 364-378.

Hamilton, J.D. and A. Herrera. "Oil Shocks and Aggregate Macroeconomic Behavior: The Role of Monetary Policy." *Journal of Money, Credit, and Banking* 36 (2004), 265-286.

Hansen, P.R. and A. Lunde. "A Forecast Comparison of Volatility Models: Does Anything Beat a GARCH(1,1)?" *Journal of Applied Econometrics* 20 (2005), 873-889.

Henry, C. "Investment Decisions under Uncertainty: The Irreversibility Effect." *American Economic Review* 64 (1974), 1006-12.

Herrera, A.M. and E. Pesavento. "Oil Price Shocks, Systematic Monetary Policy, and the 'Great Moderation'." *Macroeconomic Dynamics* 13 (2009), 107-137.

Herrera, A.M., L.G. Lagalo, and T. Wada. "Oil Price Shocks and Industrial Production: Is the Relationship Linear?" *Macroeconomic Dynamics* 15 (Supplement 3) (2011), 472-497.

Hooker, M.A. "What Happened to the Oil Price-Macroeconomy Relationship?" *Journal of Monetary Economics* 38 (1996), 195-213.

Jarque, C.M. and A.K. Bera. "Efficient Tests for Normality, Homoscedasticity, and Serial Independence of Regression Residuals." *Economics Letters* 6 (1980), 255-259.

Kellogg, R. "The Effect of Uncertainty on Investment: Evidence from Texas Oil Drilling." NBER Working Paper #16541 (2010).

Kilian, L. "The Economic Effects of Energy Price Shocks." *Journal of Economic Literature* 46 (2008), 871-909.

Kilian, L. "Not All Oil Price Shocks Are Alike: Disentangling Demand and Supply Shocks in the Crude Oil Market." *American Economics Review* 99 (2009a), 1053-1069.

Kilian, L. Comment on "Causes and Consequences of the Oil Shock of 2007-08." *Brookings Papers on Economic Activity* 1 (2009b), 267-278.

Kilian, L. and L.T. Lewis. "Does the Fed Respond to Oil Price Shocks?" *The Economic Journal* 121 (2011), 1047-1072.

Kilian, L. and R.J. Vigfusson. "Nonlinearities in the Oil Price-Output Relationship." *Macroeconomic Dynamics* 15 (Supplement 3) (2011a), 337-363.

Kilian, L. and R. Vigfusson. "Are the Responses of the U.S. Economy Asymmetric in Energy Price Increases and Decreases?" *Quantitative Economics* 2 (2011b), 419-453.

Kim, I.M. and P. Loungani. "The Role of Energy in Real Business Cycle Models." *Journal of Monetary Economics* 29 (1992), 173-189.

Koop, G, M.H. Pesaran, and S.M. Potter. "Impulse Response Analysis in Nonlinear Multivariate Models." *Journal of Econometrics* 74 (1996), 119-147.

Kroner, K.F. and V.K. Ng. "Modeling Asymmetric Comovements of Asset Returns." *Review of Financial Studies* 11 (1998), 817-844.

Kwiatkowski, D., P.C.B. Phillips, P. Schmidt, and Y. Shin. "Testing the Null Hypothesis of Stationarity Against the Alternative of a Unit Root." *Journal of Econometrics* 54 (1992), 159-178.

Lee, K. and S. Ni. "On the Dynamic Effects of Oil Price Shocks: A Study Using Industry Level Data." *Journal of Monetary Economics* 49 (2002), 823-852.

Lee, K., W. Kang, and R.A. Ratti. "Oil Price Shocks, Firm Uncertainty and Investment." *Macroeconomic Dynamics* 15 (Supplement 3) (2011), 416-436.

Lee, K., S. Ni, and R.A. Ratti. "Oil Shocks and the Macroeconomy: The Role of Price Variability." *The Energy Journal* 16 (1995), 39-56.

Ljung, T. and G. Box. "On a Measure of Lack of Fit in Time Series Models." *Biometrica* 66 (1979), 66-72.

Majd, S. and R.S. Pindyck. "Time to Build, Option Value, and Investment Decisions." *Journal of Financial Economics* 18 (1987), 7-27.

Mandelbrot, B.B. "The Variation of Certain Speculative Prices." *Journal of Business* 36 (1963), 394-419.

Mork, K.A. "Oil and the Macroeconomy When Prices Go Up and Down: An Extension of Hamilton's Results." *Journal of Political Economy* 91 (1989), 740-744.

Nelson, D.B. "Conditional Heteroscedasticity in Asset Returns." *Econometrica* 59 (1991), 347-370.

Pagan, A. "Econometric Issues in the Analysis of Regressions with Generated Regressors." *International Economic Review* 25 (1984), 221–247.

Pindyck, R.H. "Irreversibility, Uncertainty, and Investment." *Journal of Economic Literature* 29 (1991), 110-148.

Potter, S.M. "Nonlinear Impulse Response Functions." *Journal of Economic Dynamics and Control* 24 (2000), 1425-1446.

Rahman, S. and A. Serletis. "The Asymmetric Effects of Oil Price Shocks." *Macroeconomic Dynamics* 15 (Supplement 3) (2011), 437-471.

Rahman, S. and A. Serletis. "Oil Price Uncertainty and the Canadian Economy: Evidence from a VARMA, GARCH-in-Mean, Asymmetric BEKK Model." *Energy Economics* 34 (2012), 603-610.

Rotemberg, J.J. and M. Woodford. "Imperfect Competition and the Effects of Energy Price Increases on Economic Activity." *Journal of Money, Credit, and Banking* 28 (1996), 549-577.

Rubin, J. and P. Buchanan. "What's the Real Cause of the Global Recession?" CIBC World Markets *Report* (2008), 4-6.

Schwert, W. "Stock Volatility and Crash of 87." *Review of Financial Studies* 3 (1989), 77-102.

Shields, K., N. Olekalns, Ó.T. Henry, and C. Brooks. "Measuring the Response of Macroeconomic Uncertainty to Shocks." *Review of Economics and Statistics* 87 (2005), 362-370.

Silvennoinen, A. and T. Teräsvirta. "Multivariate GARCH Models." In T.G. Andersen, R.A. Davis, J.-P. Kreiss, and T. Mikosch (Eds.), *Handbook of Financial Time Series*. New York: Springer (2011).

Taylor, S. *Modeling Financial Time Series*. New York: John Wiley & Sons (1986).

Triantis, A.J. and J.E. Hodder. "Valuing Flexibility as a Complex Option." *Journal of Finance* 45 (1990), 549-566.

Tsay, R.S. *Analysis of Financial Time Series*. New York: John Wiley & Sons (2010).

Tse, Y.K. and A.K.C. Tsui. "A Multivariate GARCH Model with Time-Varying Correlations." *Journal of Business and Economic Statistics* 20 (2002), 351-362.

van Dijk, D., P.H. Franses, and H.P. Boswijk. "Absorption of Shocks in Nonlinear Autoregressive Models." *Computational Statistics and Data Analysis* 51 (2007), 4206-4226.

Zakoïan, J.M. "Threshold Heteroscedastic Models." *Journal of Economic Dynamics and Control* 18 (1994), 931-944.

Subject Index

Author Index